"The authors have built on the pillars of classic, educationally sound theories to create an umbrella that synthesizes all of the theories into a usable format. Practical ways to influence the mental state of the learners is clearly addressed. Quantum Teaching always focuses on "what makes sense to the learner.""

— Michael Grinder
Author, *Righting the Educational Conveyor Belt* and
ENVoy, Your Personal Guide to Classroom Management

"Hooray! Finally a book that is practical, readable, timely and that offers hands-on ideas grounded in sound research and theory. This is a book for me to learn from and also a book for my son – in his fourth year of teaching."

— Robert Garmston, Ed.D.
Professor Emeritus, California State University, Sacramento
Co-Director, Institute for Intelligent Behavior

"Want to raise student achievement? Want to reach *every* student? Want a practical 'do-it-tomorrow' guide that incorporates all the latest findings to enthuse students? This is it."

— Colin Rose
Co-Author, *Accelerated Learning for the 21st Century*

"This book is full of specific techniques for developing a respectful, mutually empowering learning environment regardless of the curriculum content. It is exactly what is needed for teacher preparation and renewal."

— Barbara K. Given, Ph.D.
George Mason University

"An excellent resource for teachers. Provides both the background and strategies to boost learning and make teaching more fun."

— Eric Jensen
Author, *Brain-Based Learning*

"In today's classroom, orchestrating student success is even more challenging than ever before. *Quantum Teaching* gives you the pathway to help lead your students and you to greater heights. Oh, yes!"

— Kevin T. Irvine
Colorado Teacher of the Year

QUANTUM TEACHING
Orchestrating Student Success

Bobbi DePorter   •   Mark Reardon   •   Sarah Singer-Nourie

ALLYN AND BACON
Boston • London • Toronto • Sydney • Tokyo • Singapore

To all the committed teachers who make a positive difference in the lives of students. May your teaching be exciting, inspiring and rewarding as you dynamically impact your students' success.

Edited by Mike Hernacki

Designed by Linus Saint James

Copyright illustrations by Ellen Duris Gastaldo

Additional illustrations by Colin Nourie

Series Editor: Frances Helland
Editorial Assistant: Bridget Keane
Marketing Manager: Brad Parkins
Cover Administrator: Linda Knowles
Manufacturing Buyer: Suzanne Lareau
Cover Designer: Suzanne Harbison

Copyright © 1999 by Allyn & Bacon
A Viacom Company
160 Gould St.
Needham Heights, MA 02194

Internet: www.abacon.com
America Online: College Online

ISBN 0-205-28664-X

Printed in the United States of America

10 9 8 7 6 5 4 3 2   02 01 00 99 98

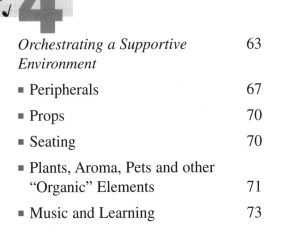

We thank the following educational pioneers for their contribution to us all:

Dr. Thomas Armstrong, Richard Bandler, Tony Buzan, Renate Nummela Caine, Geoffrey Caine, Dr. Antonio R. Damasio, Robert Dilts, Dr. L. Freeman Dhority, Dr. Emile Donchin, Dr. Howard Gardner, Dr. Michael Gazziniga, Dr. William Glasser, Daniel Goleman, John Grinder, Michael Grinder, Kurt Hahn, Leslie Hart, Dr. Ned Herrmann, Dr. Madeline Hunter, D.W. Johnson & R.T. Johnson, Susan Kovalik, Dr. Georgi Lozanov, Dr. Paul MacLean, Dr. Dawna Markova, Dr. Roger Sperry, Dr. Robert Sylwester and Dr. Pat Wolfe.

We acknowledge these professional innovators in education and learning:

Rob Abernathy, Stan Adams, Carole Allen, Rich Allen, Vicki Au, Brian Blackstock, Scott Bornstein, Chris Brewer, Linda Brown-Schaeff, Don Campbell, Linda MacRae Campbell, Glenn Capelli, Michael Carr, Libyan Labiosa-Cassone, Philip Cassone, Dr. Charles Connolly, Dee Dickinson, Gordon Dryden, Carol Maero-Fetzer, Dr. Robert Garmston, Michael Gelb, Dr. Barbara Given, Dr. John Grassi, Dr. Carla Hannaford, Merrill Harmin, DC Harrison, Eric Jensen, Robert Kiyosaki, Diane Loomans, Doug McPhee, Kate Neale, David Neenan, Dr. Ann Nevin-Parta, Dr. Nancy Omaha Boy, Dr. Lyelle Palmer, Bob Pike, Anthony Robbins, Colin Rose, Dr. Donald Schuster, Blair Singer, Steve Snyder, Tony Stockwell, Josephine Tan, Marshall Thurber, Dr. Jeannette Vos, Maggie Weiss and Joyce Wycoff.

We thank all the innovative facilitators within Learning Forum, in particular:

David Clarke, Gayle Copeland, Greg Evans, Joe Hedgecock, Jan Hensley, Tricia Huppert, Kevin Irvine, John LeTellier, Kim Mason, Tom Pew and Sandy Rasnake.

To those who were part of the initial development of Quantum Teaching, we appreciate your risk and feedback:

Peter Anderson, Principal, Northwood Middle School, Woodstock School District, Woodstock, Illinois; Emily Barton, Title One Coordinator, El Cajon Valley High School, and Karen Skullerud, Helix High School, Grossmont Union High School District, La Mesa, California; and JoAnn Evans, Assistant Superintendent, Thornton Township High Schools District 205, South Holland, Illinois.

Thanks to all those teachers and administrators who are implementing Quantum Teaching day in and day out, in particular:

> Lori Brickley and Ken Ozuna, Rancho Bernardo High School, San Diego, California; Marguerite Owens and Matt Wesley, Northwood Middle School, Woodstock, Illinois; Mark Essay, Arthur Meighen High School, Portage La Prairie, Manitoba; The Acceleration Team at Thornton Township High Schools, South Holland, Illinois, and in particular, Patti Brucki; Jeanie Pugh, Doug Hartung, and Barbara Kent, El Cajon Valley High School, El Cajon, California; Kevin Osborne, Tia Robinson, Larry Oedewaldt and Julie McGuffin, Helix High School, La Mesa, California; Annette Stamos, Bill Madigan, Adrienne Harber, Bob Raymond, Armando Cunanan and Ona Elliott, Mt. Miguel High School, Spring Valley, California; Julie Jasper, Sandburg Middle School, Glendora, California; Stacey Holder, John Sinnott Elementary School, Milpitas, California; and Stacy Kuehnis, Los Gatos High School, Los Gatos, California.

To Mike Singleton at Motorola Inc. and to Larry and Kellie Hartstein, thank you for your support and belief in Quantum Teaching.

This project was clearly a team effort. Although we all had a hand in nearly all aspects of this book, each made a distinct and valuable contribution.

> We especially thank Mike Hernacki for his invaluable writing expertise and guidance. You made it sing! We appreciate the talents of Linus Saint James for design and graphics; Ellen Duris Gastaldo for her design consultation and illustrations; Colin Nourie for his illustrations; Shelby Reeder for researching and editing; the Learning Forum staff, and in particular Lynn Flanders, Sean McGrath and Lori-anne Cash for their assistance; and to our publicist, Andrea Nordstrom Caughey, our literary agent, Sandra Dijkstra, along with associates, Rita Holm and Sandra Zane, and our editor at Allyn and Bacon, Frances Helland, along with marketing associate, Kate Sheehan, much gratitude for their support.

And with deep appreciation to our spouses, Joe Chapon, Lynn Reardon and Colin Nourie. You can have us back now!

QUANTUM TEACHING

Orchestrating Student Success

Orchestrating Student Success

Welcome

to the world of Quantum Teaching!

If you teach, design lessons, create trainings or in any other way interact with students in a learning situation, Quantum Teaching is for you, and this book is your guide to becoming a Quantum Teacher.

What if

you had the secrets of the world's master teachers, presenters and facilitators?

What if you had the best classroom applications from current research about how the brain learns?

You hold in your hands a wealth of knowledge – a treasure chest of philosophies, models and strategies – and as you combine them with your natural abilities, your teaching and your students' learning will improve.

Take a moment and imagine the place where you teach – a classroom, lecture hall, the gym floor – the place where your students learn. Hear the hum of focused, interested, participating students. Notice hands raised in anticipation, bodies leaning forward full of curiosity, and acts of celebration. Hear the joy of insights shared and the warmth of encouraging words. Glance around at a place that speaks of learning and exploration. Look into your students' eyes, feel the influence you have in their lives.

This might be an accurate description of your present classroom. Or it might be a distant dream. Regardless of your current effectiveness, the distinctions discussed in this book enhance teaching performance and student achievement. *Quantum Teaching* shows you how to be a better teacher. (The simple fact that you have this book is a solid indication of your dedication to teaching, and that you want to be a better teacher.) *Quantum Teaching* illustrates how to facilitate learning artfully and purposefully, regardless of the subject matter you teach. Using the Quantum Teaching methodology, you'll be able to synthesize powerful distinctions about learning into lessons that propel student performance.

Learning in living color!

The teaching/learning process is a complex phenomenon. Everything counts – every word, thought, action and association – and to the degree that you orchestrate the environment, the presentation and the design is the degree to which learning occurs (Lozanov, 1978). Quantum Teaching is the orchestration of learning in living color, in "surround sound," with all the nuances. It factors in the connections, interactions and distinctions that maximize the moment of learning.

Quantum Teaching focuses on the dynamic relationships within the classroom environment – the interactions that build the foundations and frameworks for learning.

Quantum Teaching got its start in SuperCamp, an accelerated Quantum Learning program produced by Learning Forum, an international education company emphasizing the development of academic and personal skills (DePorter, 1992). In this 10-day residential program, students from the ages of nine to 24 acquire tools that aid them in note-taking, memory, speed reading, writing, creativity, communication and building relationships – tools that enhance their ability to gain mastery in their lives. Results show students who attend SuperCamp raise their grades, participate more and feel better about themselves (Vos-Groenendal, 1991).

Quantum Teaching is the body of knowledge and methodology used in the design, presentation and facilitation of SuperCamp. Founded on such educationally-sound theories as Accelerated Learning (Lozanov), Multiple Intelligences (Gardner), Neuro-Linguistic Programming (Grinder and Bandler), Experiential Learning (Hahn), Socratic Inquiry, Cooperative Learning (Johnson and Johnson), and Elements of Effective Instruction (Hunter), Quantum Teaching weaves the best of the best into a multi-sensory, multi-intelligence, brain-compatible package, boosting teachers' ability to inspire and students' ability to achieve. A fresh, alive, applicable and practical approach to learning, Quantum Teaching offers a synthesis of what you're looking for: new ways to maximize the impact of your teaching efforts through the development of relationships, the orchestration of learning and the delivery of curriculum. This methodology is based on 18 years of experience and research with over 25,000 students, and the synergy of hundreds of teachers.

Quantum Teaching includes specific guidelines for creating an effective learning environment, designing curriculum, delivering content and facilitating the learning process. As you absorb the contents of this book, you'll gain ways to increase:

SuperCamp Results

- 68% INCREASE MOTIVATION
- 73% IMPROVE GRADES
- 81% DEVELOP MORE CONFIDENCE
- 84% INCREASE SELF-ESTEEM
- 98% CONTINUE TO USE SKILLS

- participation by orchestrating state,
- motivation and interest by applying the design frame known by the acronym "EEL Dr. C,"
- sense of community by employing the 8 Keys of Excellence,
- retention by utilizing "SLIM-n-BIL,"
- your students' listening skills by following the Principles of Powerful Communication,
- the elegance of transitions with "IBA."

These, along with many other strategies, put you and your students on the fast track to learning success.

To facilitate your understanding of Quantum Teaching's philosophy, here are a few key words and our definitions. These will make more sense to you as you learn the concepts and strategies introduced in this book; for now they'll provide some scaffolding on which to hang new concepts.

Quantum: Interactions that transform energy into radiance. Quantum Teaching, therefore, is the orchestration of the variety of interactions that exist in and around the moment of learning. These interactions include elements for effective learning that affect student success. These interactions transform the students' natural talents and abilities into radiance that benefits themselves and others.

Accelerated Learning: Removing the barriers that impede the natural process of learning through the conscious use of music, peripherals, appropriate materials, presentation and "active engagement."

Facilitation: To make easy. When we use this word we mean the implementation of strategies that remove the barriers to learning, thus returning the process of learning to its natural, "easy" state.

The Prime Directive

Quantum Teaching rests on this concept: *Theirs to Ours, Ours to Theirs.* It is the Prime Directive, the foundational premise behind the strategies, models and beliefs.

All that's done within the framework of Quantum Teaching – every interaction with students, every design of the curriculum, every instructional method – sets squarely on the principle of *Theirs to Ours, Ours to Theirs.*

Here's what it means. Theirs to Ours, Ours to Theirs reminds us of the importance of entering the students' world *first.* In order for you to earn the right to teach, you must first build authentic bridges into your students' lives. A teaching credential or a document stating you can teach or train merely says you have the *authority* to teach. It doesn't mean you have the *right* to teach. Teaching someone is an *earned* right, and is granted by the student, not by the state Department of Education. Learning by its very definition is a full-contact activity. In other words, learning involves all aspects of the human personality – thoughts, feelings and body language – in addition to prior knowledge, attitudes and beliefs and perception of the future. Therefore, since learning deals with the entire person, the right to facilitate that learning must be granted by the learner and earned by the teacher.

So, first, enter their world. Why? It earns you the permission to lead/guide/facilitate their journey into expanded awareness and knowledge. How? By associating what you teach with an event, thought or feeling extracted from their home, social, athletic, musical, artistic, recreational or academic lives. Once this link has been established, then you can bring

Enter your students' world!

them into your world, and give them your understanding of the content. This is where new vocabulary, mental models, formulas, etc. are unveiled. As connections and interactions are explored, both the students and teacher gain new understanding and "ours" broadens to include not only the class but also the teacher. Finally, with this expanded understanding and greater mastery, the students can take what they've learned into their world and apply it to new situations. *Theirs to Ours, Ours to Theirs*. It is the way of human dynamics. It is the prime directive of Quantum Teaching.

The Tenets

Quantum Teaching also embodies five tenets, or resident truths. Similar in scope to the prime directive, Theirs to Ours, the tenets permeate all aspects of Quantum Teaching. Think of them as the basic chord structure of your learning symphony. The tenets are:

■ **Everything Speaks**
Everything from your classroom environment to your body language, from the handouts you distribute to the design of your lesson; everything is sending a message about learning.

■ **Everything Is On Purpose**
Everything that happens under your orchestration has an intended purpose . . . everything.

■ **Experience Before Label**
Our brains thrive on complex stimulation. It drives the need to know. Therefore, learning happens best when students experience the information before they acquire the labels for what they learned.

■ **Acknowledge Every Effort**
Learning involves risking, stepping out of what

is comfortable. As students take these steps, they are acknowledged for both their competence and their confidence.

■ If It's Worth Learning, It's Worth Celebrating!

banner

(Celebration is the breakfast of champion learners.) Celebration provides feedback regarding progress and increases positive emotional associations with the learning.

You'll become very familiar with these tenets as you traverse the following pages. Let them act as the infrastructure for your model of education.

The Quantum Teaching Model

The Quantum Teaching Model is much like a symphony. When you attend the symphony, many elements factor into your musical experience. We can put those elements into two categories: context and content.

The **context** is the setting for your experience. It's the grandeur of the orchestra hall itself (the environment), the passion of the conductor and musicians (the atmosphere), the balance of the instruments and musicians working together (the foundation), and the maestro's crafted interpretation of the score (the design). These elements blend together, creating the entire musical experience.

The other part, **content,** is distinct and equally as important as the context. Think of the musical score itself as the content, the actual notes on the page. And there's more to it than notes on a page. One element of the content is how each musical phrase is played (the presentation). The content also includes the maestro's masterful facilitation of the orchestra, tapping the musical talent of each musician and the potential in each instrument.

The magic of the experience unfolds because the context is in place, allowing the music to come alive. As you orchestrate the success of your students, the same elements are in place: atmosphere, environment, foundation, design, presentation and facilitation.

The Format of this Book

Quantum Teaching, the book, is divided into these two main sections: context and content. Just like the symphonic experience, you, as the conductor of your students' learning, have many pieces to orchestrate. We've organized these pieces into the following chapters:

In the **context** section, you'll find all the pieces you need to orchestrate:

- An Empowering Atmosphere

- A Strong Foundation

- A Supportive Environment

- A Dynamic Learning Design

In the **content** section, you'll find the delivery skills for any curriculum, in addition to the strategies your students need to take responsibility for their learning:

- Powerful Presentation

- Elegant Facilitation

- Learning-to-Learn Skills

- Life Skills

As you scan the book, you'll notice images, icons and illustrations to highlight the important concepts. For example, "Maestro" is your conductor, highlighting important ideas as you read the musical score of *Quantum Teaching*. As you read more closely you'll find examples, anecdotes and stories that amplify the information and apply what you're learning to everyday educational situations. The flip-chart captures key points, while the 'action' slate directs you to take action. You'll even notice opportunities for you to reflect and record your insights.

Designed and written as an interactive textbook, *Quantum Teaching* is meant to feel like a helpful companion. Each chapter is written using the Principles of Powerful Communication, fortified by a multi-sensory, multi-intelligence approach, and crafted to Quantum Teaching's Learning Design Frame known as "EEL Dr. C."

Quantum Teaching models its teaching philosophy and strategies with "Maestro" in the margins, reminding you of the Design Frame components while you read through the chapter. Here's a quick look at EEL Dr. C and what it means.

make chart

■ **Enroll**
Creates buy-in by addressing "What's In It For Me" (WIIFM), and taps into the learner's life.

■ **Experience**
Creates or elicits a common experience to which all learners can relate.

■ **Label**
Provides the key words, concepts, models, formulas, strategies; the "input."

■ **Demonstrate**
Provides opportunities for the learner to "show that they know."

■ **Review** */reflect*
Provides the learner with ways to review the material and solidify that, "I know that I know this." *written*
"buddy buzz"

■ **Celebrate**
An acknowledgment of completion, participation and acquisition of skills and knowledge.

To get the most out of this book, engage fully with the text. Allow yourself to participate. Write on the pages, and/or keep a notebook of what you'll use and exactly how you'll use it. Be an excellent learner, and notice how quickly the strategies and techniques become woven into your personal teaching repertoire.

We firmly believe that you, the teacher, are a powerful determinant in student success. Dr. Georgi Lozanov, Bulgarian researcher and founder of suggestology, methods also known collectively as accelerated learning, points to your unmistakable influence (Lozanov, 1978). Dr. Michael Gazzaniga concurs, "Nature's biological imperative is simple. No ability or skill will unfold until or unless given the appropriate model environment" (Gazzaniga, 1992). You're a significant factor in the learning environment and the lives of your students. Therefore, your role stretches beyond that of knowledge-giver. You're a fellow learner, a model, a guide, a facilitator – indeed, the orchestrator of student success!

A final note as you begin your symphonic adventure. We believe in you. As fellow educators, we know the level of commitment and dedication it takes to teach today's students. We applaud your efforts and trust that these pages simply enhance your existing greatness. Welcome to the world of Quantum Teaching!

Celebrate! *The Adventure Begins!*

Orchestrating Success Through Context

SETTING THE STAGE

Everything in your classroom literally "speaks," setting the stage for learning. Every detail says something—about you and your attitudes toward teaching and learning. Your classroom environment is loaded with cues, and consciously or unconsciously, students pick up on them. These cues color the students' expectations and ultimately, their entire learning experience. That's why it's vital to listen to what your classroom is saying about learning and turn it to your advantage.

Part I

With the help of this book, you'll learn how to transform your classroom into a "learning community" – a society-in-miniature where every detail has been carefully orchestrated to support optimum learning – from the way you arrange your desks, to classroom policies, to the design of the lesson.

In orchestrating the details, you're setting a context in which your students' future learning will take place. You want that context to be positive, supportive and inviting. You want your learning community to be a place that fosters awareness, listening, participation, feedback and growth. A place where emotions are respected. An environment in which students can move into resourceful states, are willing to be accountable, and can trust one another. A place with no limits to what can be accomplished.

Your classroom can be a "home" where students are not only open to feedback, but also seek it; where they learn to acknowledge and support others; where they experience joy and satisfaction, giving and receiving, learning and growing.

Context sets the stage for learning, and has four aspects: atmosphere, foundation, environment and design.

Your classroom's **atmosphere** includes the languaging you choose, rapport with students, and your attitudes about school and learning. A joyful atmosphere puts the joy in learning.

Foundation is the framework: the shared purpose, beliefs, agreements, policies, procedures and rules that give you and your students the guidelines for operating within your learning community.

The **environment** is the way you construct your classroom: lighting, color, arrangement of desks and chairs, plants and music – everything that supports learning.

Design is the purposeful crafting of essential elements that create student buy-in, increased meaning and better transfer.

What is your classroom saying?

great. &
mission
statement

When these four aspects are carefully orchestrated, something magical happens. The context itself actually creates a sense of belonging, which in turn fosters ownership and respect. Your classroom becomes a learning community, a place where students want to be, not a place where they're forced to go.

We invite you to take a close look at what your own classroom is like right now, then follow the guidelines in the next four chapters, and discover the power of context in your world.

Orchestrating An Empowering Atmosphere

ENROLL

What if

students took steps beyond what they thought possible?

What if you could keep students engaged in their learning longer, unleash their motivation and cause their learning to occur naturally as an extension of their experience?

Imagine . . . It's the first day of school, and as Colin hurries toward his classroom, his heart races with anticipation, yet hesitation. Fear, yet excitement. Elation, yet – what? As he approaches your

EXPERIENCE

classroom, a flood of pictures, sounds and feelings fly through his brain as he wonders, "What will this year be like?"

These first moments of class tell him everything about you, your subject, your style, whether this class will seem to last a few seconds or an eternity – and of course, whether he'll succeed or fail.

What will this school year be like? Will it be "school as usual"? Or will Colin discover a place full of wonder, excitement, intrigue and respect?

Research shows that classroom social environment, or atmosphere, is one of the chief psychological determinants of academic learning (Walberg and Greenberg, 1997). Atmosphere – how a space feels, the ambience – represents the affective domain of learning. Take your favorite restaurant. You probably enjoy not only the quality of the food but also the atmosphere – calm or exciting, warm or stark, traditional or contemporary. It makes your dining an *experience* rather than just another meal. You can create a similar effect with your *learning* environment as readily as the restaurant does with your eating environment. You can make it just another class or an outstanding experience of discovery. The choice is yours. Key ingredients for superb atmosphere are intention, rapport, joy and wonder, risk-taking, belonging and modeling.

LABEL

ⓐ THE HIDDEN POWER OF INTENTION

A teacher's intention, or belief about a student's ability and motivation, speaks loud and clear. Think back to the last time you taught. How did your intention (positive or negative) come through? Did you believe and act as if students wanted

> "People's beliefs about their abilities have a profound effect on those abilities"
>
> — *Albert Bandura, 1988*

to be their best – that they can succeed, want to succeed and will succeed? Did you see through the image students project, and tap into what you know waits inside – their best selves? Did you interact with students while maintaining a positive intention about who they are and what they can be, and watch them rise to your expectations? All of these are evidence of your intention. And they count for as much or more than anything you say.

Everything Speaks

Students "get" your intention faster and more accurately than they "get" anything you teach. Practice consciously changing your intention by imagining a "10" (as in a scale from one to 10) printed on each student's forehead. Or maybe it's easier for you to "see" a gold star on each forehead, as if they're all top students. Interact with each one this way, and notice the difference it makes.

In working with many teachers at different levels, we've noticed an interesting, yet troubling pattern in their interactions with students in "high ability" groups versus "low ability" groups. With the high ability groups, teachers tend to smile more, engage at a more personal and conversational level, and speak in a more intellectual and humorous manner, using complex vocabulary and acting more maturely. With the "low ability" groups, the same teachers tend to speak louder and slower (as if the students can't hear), use basic vocabulary and immature syntax, smile less, and interact at a more instructional, authoritarian level. In essence, the teachers treat the students just as their labels dictate – as high or low academic performers.

Nine out of 10 teachers say they can recall many times when they prejudged a student's failure based on his or her past behavior, and the result they got matched their expectations. Does the teacher's intention have an impact on the students' performance and self-image? Absolutely!

University of Pennsylvania psychologist Martin Seligman found that some people react more sensitively to this prejudging than others. In experiments, he tested swimmers to determine their personal optimism and pessimism levels (how they tended to interpret feedback). He found that some swimmers, who had tested pessimistic, when given false bad times, did even worse with further attempts. While others, who had tested optimistic, despite the negative feedback, performed better (Seligman, 1991).

In their book, *Education on the Edge of Possibility,* Renate Nummela Caine and Geoffrey Caine state,

> Teachers' beliefs in and about human potential and in the ability of all children to learn and achieve are critical. These aspects of the teachers' mental models have a profound impact on the learning climate and learner states of mind that teachers create. Teachers need to understand that students' feelings and attitudes will be involved and will profoundly influence student learning (Caine and Caine, 1977, p. 124).

Role of Emotions in Learning

Getting in touch with your students' emotions can help you get them into learning faster. Drawing on their emo-

Teresa had a reputation in school of being a disruptive, angry troublemaker. She was kicked out of classes daily for arguing with teachers, mouthing off and picking fights with other students. She frequently found herself on the suspension list, and was failing many classes. Despite all that, her teacher, Miss Singer, chose to believe in her doggedly and reaffirm it constantly, despite Teresa's own lack of belief in herself.

In the first semester, Teresa made many choices based on her old pattern. As a result, Miss Singer often kicked her out of class, and held many conferences with her and her father. In fact, she eventually failed the class. However, Miss Singer never let her off the hook.

So how was this different from all of her other classes? Miss Singer continued to hold the line with her, not based on her being a "problem", but based on the "10" she knew Teresa could be. Teresa knew how this teacher felt, and a rapport developed. Miss Singer established a relationship with Teresa by making an investment in who she was. While in the moments of each incident, Teresa felt angry and frustrated (as we all are in hard life lessons), but the teacher left her each time with compassion and the unswerving belief that she knew Teresa could do it. Here's an excerpt from a note Teresa left:

> Dear Miss Singer,
> Earlier this year, I thought I wasn't going to make it because we had some problems. But we made it through thick and thin. You helped me to believe in myself. At first I didn't, but now I do. I hope my next teacher will be as good as you. Thank you for everything you did and taught me....I'm sorry for all I put you through. I was surprised that you didn't kick me out of your class [permanently] because I know I was a pain. Now I'm determined to get something out of life. My mom [deceased] would be proud of me for doing this and I'm going to make her happy.
> Love,
>
> Teresa
> P.S.- Thanks for believing in me. And keep up the good work because what you're doing is helping a lot of students get through life.

tions also makes the learning more meaningful and permanent.

Think back for a moment to when you attended college. In which class do you remember being more engaged in the subject? What information do you remember better – the information you got from the professor you liked, or from the one you didn't care for? Right! The professor you liked created in you an emotional buy-in to the learning, which cemented the subject into your memory.

Increasingly, brain research shows connections between emotional engagement, long-term memory and learning. Researcher and cognitive psychologist, Dr. Daniel Goleman explains:

> In the dance of feeling and thought the emotional faculty guides our moment-to-moment decisions, working hand-in-hand with the rational mind, enabling – or disabling – thought itself. In a sense we have two brains, two minds – and two different kinds of intelligence: rational and emotional. How we do in life (and learning) is determined by both – it is not just IQ, but emotional intelligence that matters. Indeed, intellect cannot work at its best without emotional intelligence (Goleman, 1995, p. 28).

Research tells us that without emotional engagement, the brain's neural activity is less than what it needs to be to make the learning "stick" in the memory (Goleman, 1995, LeDoux, 1993, MacLean, 1990).

Have you ever wondered why learners shut down and can't hear you, why you momentarily lose your sanity when you get angry, or why you always think of your best comebacks an hour after you've been insulted? We now know, thanks to the work of Dr. Paul MacLean, Dr. Joseph LeDoux and Dr. Daniel Goleman, that when the brain perceives threat or distress, its neural capacity to reason rationally is minimized. The brain is "emotionally hijacked" (Goleman, 1995) into the fight-or-flight mode and operates at survival level. The availability of neural connections and activity actually decreases or becomes minimized in this situation, and the brain cannot access Higher Order Thinking Skills (HOTS). This phenomenon, known as "downshifting," is a psychophysiological response, and can halt learning in the moment and over time (McLean, 1990). Your students' ability to learn actually decreases.

Downshifting

The good news is, the brain can also do the opposite. With positive stress, or supportive pressure, known as "eustress," the brain can emotionally engage, and allow for the maximizing of neural activity. Mihaly Csikszentmihalyi is the University of Chicago psychologist well known for his research in documenting a state called "flow," which he defines as "the state in which people are so involved in an activity that nothing else seems to matter (Csikszentmihalyi, 1990, p. 4)." He describes the relationship between eustress and flow this way:

> People seem to concentrate best when the demands on them are a bit greater than usual, and they are able to give more than usual. If there is too little demand on them, people are bored. If there is too much for them to handle, they get anxious. Flow occurs in that delicate zone between boredom and anxiety (Goleman, 1992).

Harvard psychologist and researcher Howard Gardner, best known for developing the theory of multiple intelligences, says this about flow:

> We should use kids' positive states to draw them into learning in the domains where they can develop competencies. . . . Flow is an internal state that signifies a kid is engaged in a task that's right. You have to find something you like and stick to it. It's when kids get bored in school that they fight and act up, and when they're overwhelmed by a challenge that they get anxious about their schoolwork. But you learn at your best when you have something you care about and you can get pleasure from being engaged in. (Gardner, 1995, p. 94)

The key is building that emotional buy-in, putting fun into the learning, creating a relationship and removing all threat from the learning atmosphere. Like a car, you want the learning process running on all cylinders, so you start in first gear (removing threat) and work up to HOTS from there.

Studies show that students learn more when their classes are satisfying, challenging and friendly and they have a voice in decision-making. Under such conditions, students engaged more often in non-required activities related to the subject matter (Walberg, 1997). This raises the stakes

"By separating emotion from logic and reason in the classroom, we've simplified school management and evaluation, but we've also then separated two sides of one coin – and lost something important in the process. It's impossible to separate emotion from the other important activities of life. Don't try . . . ."

Dr. Robert Sylwester, 1995
A Celebration of Neurons

of relationship and trust-building in teaching. With a direct correlation between emotional engagement and student learning performance, it's no longer just a warm and fuzzy idea to make everyone feel good. It's now essential to propel and cement learning.

In addition to insuring more learning and engagement for your students, emotional buy-in also dramatically affects their memory and recall of the subject matter learned. Neuroscientist Dr. Joseph LeDoux revealed the amygdala, the emotional center of the brain, plays a tremendous role in storing memory.

> . . . amygdala arousal seems to imprint in memory most moments of emotional arousal with an added degree of strength . . . . That's why we are more likely, for example, to remember where we went on a first date, or what we were doing when we heard the news that the space shuttle Challenger had exploded. The more intense the amygdala arousal, the stronger the imprint (LeDoux, 1994).

b RAPPORT

To create emotional engagement, a teacher must build rapport. Rapport constructs an on-ramp into students' lives, creating a way to enter their world, know their concerns, share their successes and speak their language. Developing rapport can mean less work in engaging students, easier classroom management, longer focus time and more fun.

Remember:

The degree to which we enter our students' world is the degree of influence we have in their lives.

Teachers often discuss the age-old question: "Do they have to like us?" If they do, the job becomes much easier. We teachers don't have to work nearly as hard if we know the students are with us, rather than fighting us.

"Don't smile until mid-term" is bad advice, rooted in the "They don't have to like us" camp. This type of thinking ignores the research that shows teachers achieve higher results when they remove any threat, engage student emotions and build rapport. We find that even with the toughest, gang-affiliated, "unteachable" high school kids, the one thing that engages them in learning is the rapport we build with them as people.

This influence separates those who are good teachers from those who are truly inspired teachers. Develop rapport, and learners will accept you and what you have to say. Because of the relationship you develop with them, what could have been a power struggle or major disciplinary situation becomes transformed into a conversation of recommitment or agreement. In addition, when things get tough, like with the content (the part of the curriculum even you dislike), or with the context (the week before break) – or when relationships get tense to the point that you'd normally lose the students – they'll hang in with you because they trust you.

Building rapport and safety takes intention, compassion and risk on your part. This is different from the old paradigm that said, "Set the rules and regulations first, get right into the content and the relationship will build over time." The Quantum Teaching way suggests that from Day One, we get out from behind our content and policy, and just get to know the students and build rapport with them. It's part of establish-

Remember Teresa, the once-troubled student? As she attests, there is no doubt that empowering students through positive intention for their success yields great results. Despite an entire semester of bad behavior, failing grades and problems, Teresa's teacher, Miss Singer, still believed in her, and knew she could succeed. Miss Singer told her this and the next day received this note:

"... I went home and took time being introspective by myself, sorting things out. I know my apathy caused you to worry about me. But your affirmations helped me to believe that I could succeed. I've made up my mind and I'm going for it, and I feel good about myself. You accepted me for who I am instead of what I do. I appreciate that because most teachers wouldn't have done that."

As a result of this exchange, Teresa acted like a new person when she came back to repeat the course. She knew her teacher believed in her, and she succeeded. Assuming students are capable, and letting them know you believe in them, can make the difference between whether they open up to you or shut you out. It's much easier to teach to an open mind – especially if *you have* an open mind!

ing an open, effective atmosphere. In fact, take the first week (or two!) of school, despite the expense of precious time, and commit yourself to building the atmosphere in your class: team, partnership, safety, rapport, rapport, rapport. Our experience has shown that taking time during the first week of school to set a safe, warm atmosphere not only builds the context for the year, but saves you time later when it comes to classroom management and re-teaching. The message students get in the first weeks? People come FIRST here, even over content.

This level of rapport produces an added benefit: permission. When you understand your students and relate to them, it gives you permission to hold them accountable for what they say and responsible for what they do. But remember, they have the right to expect the same from you.

Opening up the communication for this kind of partnership is a win/win for you and them. It allows you to speak honestly, with love, about what you see and run less risk of the students being defensive. Why? Because you care enough to give them feedback. When you interact with students with positive intention and rapport, you can speak directly to them about what matters most – who they are and how they portray themselves. They want this from you honestly and supportively. Be careful not to abuse this privilege or use it as a tool for manipulation. In any healthy relationship, we honor and respect those we love. Do so with your students.

JOY AND WONDER

When you consciously create opportunities to bring joy into your job, it adds more fun to both teaching and learning. Joy gets students ready to learn more easily, and can even change negative attitudes.

Remember the feeling you had when you rode your two-wheeler without training wheels for the very first time? Wheeeee! That moment typified the exhilarating learning that came so frequently in your infancy and childhood. Back then

Suggestions for Building Rapport

- Treat students as equals.

- Know what students like, how they think and how they feel about what's happening in their lives.

- Imagine what they say to themselves, about themselves.

- Know what keeps them from getting what they truly want. If you don't know, ask.

- Speak the truth to them in a way they can hear it clearly and gently.

- Have fun with them.

you were a learning machine. You thrived on the original ingredients present in human learning; ingredients which created the "aha". . .

Risk + Joy = Exhilaration!

Unfortunately, at some point (often in school) that feeling of joy becomes disconnected from learning, and learning becomes a flat experience. Somewhere right around junior high, (as you were "being prepared for" hard learning in high school), you started to get bogged down by "hard work" and "taking it seriously" in school learning situations. "Listen to what you're told, don't speak until spoken to, stay in your seat, don't talk to other people . . ." all of which seemed the opposite of what learning was once all about: wonder, discovery, play, asking a million questions, getting your hands on it and, that's right . . . *joy!*

Weeeeeee!

It's not too late to turn this around for your students and bring the Wheeee! back into the learning. For many students, this might seem like a new association to this boring thing they call school. For them, learning has been tedious for too long. School has become synonymous with no-fun. You have the opportunity to reconnect your students to the wonder and joy of learning!

When you do this, you not only make teaching more joyful for yourself, you also change your students' negative attitudes and get them ready to learn.

In *The Laughing Classroom,* Loomans and Kolberg say:

Is it possible that a portion of our current discipline problems stems from a serious, heavily regulated approach to the learning process? Oftentimes it's the class clown or the disturbing student that teachers consider to be the biggest discipline problem in the classroom. And yet, the rebel and the class clown both have something significant in common: They refuse to give in to the joyless grind of learning without spontaneity and laughter. Many of their disturbances arise from their innate desire for humor and stimulation in the classroom....When the classroom is a lively, creative environment where laughter abounds, students of every age have a natural outlet where their curious minds can flourish (Loomans and Kolberg, 1993, p. 153).

Consider these three ways to inject more joy into teaching: Affirmations, Acknowledgments and Celebrations.

The Impact of Affirmations

Use affirmations as a powerful way to add more joy and reach the voice inside your head. That's right – we said the voice inside your head. You do have one. It's the one that just said, "What voice?" Otherwise known as internal dialogue (ID), it serves as a reflection of our values and beliefs and exerts a strong influence over our experience of the world at any given moment.

The voices inside your students' heads talk non-stop throughout your teaching. It's part of what happens for regular human beings, yet we often just teach right over it, ignoring it. Since it speaks all the time, the pertinent question might be, "Is that little voice supporting, interrupting or blocking the learning?" With a little forethought, you can use positive suggestions and self-affirmations to influence the restructuring of your students' identities into something positive and supportive to the student and the learning. In Chapter 4 you'll learn how to do this with the surroundings of your room.

Chapter 4
page 67

Giving (and Receiving) Acknowledgments

Another fundamental tenet of Quantum Teaching is:

Acknowledge Every Effort

Everyone likes to be acknowledged. Receiving acknowledgment fills us with pride, self-confidence and happiness. Research supports the concept of student efficacy increasing due to teacher acknowledgment. In Gordon Wells' study of children learning language, he notes:

> If children are to make the transition confidently and easily, it is important that they experience the new environment of school as an exciting and challenging one, in which the majority of their endeavors are successful and where they are given individual recognition for who they are and what they can do....Children who feel, or who are made to feel, unaccepted and incompetent may be slow to recover their self-confidence and, as a result, their ability to benefit from the enlarged opportunities for learning that school provides may be diminished or even, in extreme cases, irrevocably damaged (Wells, 1986, p. 68).

To achieve the best results with students, acknowledge every effort, not just the correct effort. As teachers, we spend much of our acknowledgement on correctness, rather than personal learning.

Why? Because as teachers, we devote much of our time to a place called "knowing." We know what we know. We know our content, we know what our students know, what they should know and what they will know. We get paid to know. Consequently, what do we acknowledge in our learners? What they know.

The dilemma occurs because our students, in the process of getting to a place called "I know!" spend most of their time in a different place, called: learning

Learning is a fluid, dynamic, risky and exciting place. There is no knowing yet. Mistakes, creativity, potential and wonder fill this place.

There's a mismatch here. Students do what you want

1+1=?

What is the cost of acknowledging correctness rather than personal learning? Let's see:

Brian's kindergarten teacher asks the class "What's one plus one?" Brian, confident he knows the right answer, can barely stay in his seat as he waves his hand frantically. The teacher finally calls on him, and he confidently smiles and answers "One plus one is three!" The teacher smiles sympathetically as she says, "No, that's incorrect. Sally, do you know the correct answer?" and moves on. Meanwhile, the other kids laugh under their breath at Brian and the whole experience leaves him a different person. Now defeated, and having learned an important lesson, he tells himself, "Don't do that again! Don't raise your hand unless you're absolutely sure you know the answer." So he doesn't, and it sticks. Early on, Brian associates acknowledgment with CORRECTness, and he keeps his learning to himself.

What other response might his teacher give that would acknowledge his effort toward learning, yet let him know his answer is incorrect? Smiling, Brian's teacher could say, "Brian, you're way ahead of us! (High-5) Three is the perfect answer to one plus TWO, which we haven't even gotten to yet. Wow, you're fast. So if one plus TWO is three, then backtracking for a second to one plus ONE, what do you think?"

Think of three students who could use encouragement. Create concrete, specific acknowledgments for each.

them to do – they try to learn. Unfortunately they're not acknowledged for this. Only when they've become knowers do they receive praise. Start acknowledging the really important part, the learning! To truly create lifelong learners, acknowledge *every* effort they make on their road to knowing. How? Take on this challenge:

Match a student's "wrong" answer with the right question as you guide them to the correct answer, kind of like playing "Jeopardy." We call this technique "matching the answer." (See the sidebar on page 29 for an example.)

Remember to give powerful, concrete acknowledgments. "Good job," "Way to go," or "Excellent," doesn't exactly communicate what she did right. Instead try, "Great use of adjectives and vivid description in that paragraph, Lynn. It really came alive," or "Way to be generous and a great team player by sharing your supplies, Lynn. Thank you." This helps the student zero in on what she did well, so she can do it again and again.

Celebrations

Providing celebrations for your students encourages them to take more ownership and initiate their own learning. It teaches them about intrinsic motivation without "incentives." Students look forward to learning, making their education into something more than just grades.

You're watching an intense professional football game. The teams work the ball back and forth. One team scores, then the other, then the first again. As the pressure mounts, you watch the teams and notice that for each completed pass, each yard gained, each sack, the players celebrate wildly; they dance, yell, pat, hug. Why? Because they know that every step counts.

Which brings us to another Quantum Teaching tenet:

If It's Worth Learning, It's Worth Celebrating!

Those professional players (in fact, championship teams of all kinds) know that each success, each step on the way to the win accelerates them when it is anchored to a celebration. So they follow every success with a celebration, solidifying or anchoring a heightened, resourceful state of performance. The high five he gets puts him back to that resourceful state. Then, the next time a player goes for a tough play, the positive association of celebration pushes him on.

Most often when we accomplish something, we just move on to the next thing, creating no special impetus to go for it again. As a teacher, you plant seeds of success, always connecting learning and celebration.

Celebration builds the desire for success. So celebrate often. Here are some fun forms of celebration we use:

- **Applause:** A tried-and-true technique, it never fails to inspire. Try variations like "round of" applause (clap in a circle).

- **Hooray! Hooray! Hooray!:** On cue, everyone hops to their feet and yells as loud as they can, "Hooray, Hooray, Hooray!" At the same time they yell, they fling their arms forward and up. This works fantastically when done in a "wave" across the room.

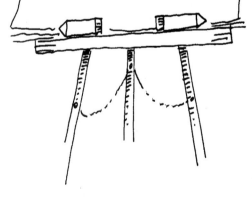

Forms of Celebration

- Applause
- Three Hoorays
- Whooshes
- Finger Snaps
- Toasts
- Public Posters
- Private Notes
- Conspiracies
- Surprises
- Strength Acknowledgments
- "Say to your neighbor . . ."
- High-5's to Neighbors
- Affirmation Statements

- **Whooshes:** On cue, everyone claps three times in unison, then sends all of their positive energy to a designated person. This looks like pushing the hands, after the claps, toward the person, yelling "whoosh" at the same time.

- **Finger Snap:** When you need a quiet acknowledgement, instead of applause, use continuous finger snaps.

- **Toasts:** Just like at a party, the whole class toasts someone, celebrating his or her doing or sharing something great (use invisible drinks and glasses).

- **Public Posters:** To acknowledge individuals or the entire class, like "3rd Period's Genius Rocks!"

- **Private Notes:** To individual students, acknowledging great efforts, contributions to class, great behavior or acts of kindness.

- **Conspiracies:** To acknowledge someone without them knowing it's coming. For example, your entire class could conspire to acknowledge another class (let's say Mrs. Brucki's class) by leaving them mysterious positive posters (or notes) that say things like, "Mrs. Brucki's class is awesome!" or "Good luck on today's test – we're behind you!" It's great to conspire for the custodians and lunch staff, too.

- **Surprises:** Like food, no homework, a period off. Make sure, however, that these surprises happen randomly. Don't make them extrinsic rewards that students begin to expect. Keep them as surprises!

- **Strength Acknowledgments:** When you want each person to get acknowledgment, after they know each other well. Have the students sit in a horseshoe shape, with one seat (the hot seat) in the open end of the horseshoe. Each person takes a turn in the hot seat. The person in that seat sits silently listening and making eye contact. Each person in the horseshoe acknowledges some special strength or quality of the person in the hot seat. The teacher can start this off so the students know how to proceed.

After a high point of learning for the entire group, try one of these. . .

- **"Say to your neighbor..."** Have each student say to the person next to her or him, "You are a fabulous speller!" (or whatever applies to what he or she just learned or demonstrated).

- **High-5's to Neighbors:** Use to acknowledge the whole group and build team, celebrating a job well done as a partner or class.

- **Affirmation Statements:** Done as a class, this celebrates the learning process. Try "We've got it," "We did it," "We're on it," and "Now we're thinking!"

WONDER

When was the last time you watched a baby? We mean *really* watched. Most adults, when they actually stop and watch usually say, "Wow." We agree.

WOW = Wide Open Wonder!

Babies are wonder machines. To them, the box their birthday toy comes in is every bit as intriguing as the gift itself, and can provide hours of fascination. Eyes widen and fingers grab at the brightly colored paper, quickly shredding it. Pulling, prying and shaking, he tests to see what this might be. Bringing it to his mouth, he tastes it to see if it's edible. Working with the lid, he learns through trial and error how to open and close the box. He may even discover how to drop the toy into the box and then dump it out. Over and over he plays these games, learning everything he can about this fascinating new object.

Everyone's original learning tool is wonder. As youngsters we allowed our genius to be unleashed every day as we explored our universe – every nook, cranny, contraption, orifice and object. Basically, we were learning machines, soaking it all in until someone said, "No." Then the natural, self-directed mechanism of wonderment slowed down, and other people started influencing our natural learning process. When we entered school, that powerful learning tool called wonder was squelched once again with right and wrong answers. Teachers imposed on us methods of "how" to learn things, which contradicted much of real-life learning.

We can bring wonder back into teaching by posing open, creative questions, opening up more than "right" answers, and answering questions with more questions (Elkind and Sweet, 1997). We can gently guide students back into their true role as learners, not just knowers. Infusing learning with wonder and exploration unleashes that genius again, adding more meaning to learning when it's initiated and sought out through wonder, curiosity, exploration and inquiry.

d RISK-TAKING

When you inject an element of risk into the learning situation, you tap into the learner's natural adventurousness. This takes them beyond their previous limits, and adds to the impact of their experience. Part of being a great learner is being a great risk-taker. More than they know, our kids spend every day taking risks. They talk to new people, boldly venture into brand new learning situations, walk into the lunch room wondering whom to sit with, and become more and more independent.

We all live in a Comfort Zone (CZ). In it we have all the things we feel comfortable with: certain activities, people, foods, places and ways of being. For example, teaching in a certain style may be in your CZ, while trying some newfangled instruction technique might be outside it. We all like to stay inside our CZ because it's easy, familiar, and yes, comfortable. Everything outside it seems dangerous, shaky and too risky.

Yet as with anything too comfortable, our CZ can become boring and stagnant. If we stay in there long enough, we run the risk of getting stuck in a rut. So we venture out to the limits of our CZ and peek out. There's that new thing waiting for us. Our little voice screams, "Don't go out there! Stay in here where it's comfy." Yet we know we must try. Though the change makes us feel weird and shaky, we try it out and accept the discomfort, knowing it will subside eventually. Sure enough, as we give it a chance, the thing that seemed so far out of our CZ now has become easy, and *voilá* . . . our CZ has expanded. That little experience represents the learning process.

Remember:

Learning is risking. Every time we adventure to learn something new, we take a big risk beyond our comfort zones.

Every time we ask our students to try something for the first time, we're asking them to take that scary step outside their comfort zones – to boldly go from a knower to learner – and that takes courage. Risk-taking keeps the brain moving, and can be exhilarating if we create a risk-safe atmosphere, full of support and the encouragement to go for it. It brings an element of challenge and "can-do" to the classroom, and creates an environment where learners take themselves beyond where they ever thought they could.

To empower your students to step outside their CZs, first start to model it yourself. You could begin with something as simple as trying a new teaching idea from this book. Share what you're doing with the students. *"Class, this next activity is one I think you'll have fun with. I'm trying it for the first time and I'm a little nervous about it. Let's explore it together."* They'll rise to the occasion. Be sure they see you going through the process

EMPOWERING STUDENTS TO STEP BEYOND COMFORT ZONES

■ Model stepping outside your comfort zone.

■ Share the idea of comfort zone with students.

■ Let students know you're supporting them 100%.

■ Enroll class in supporting one another.

What are three things you could do that are outside your current CZ?

yourself, as you invite them to take some risks.

Next, share the idea of Comfort Zone with your students, (like we just did for you, drawings and all). Let them know you'll be stepping out there too, and that learning and getting to excellence are all about stepping out of those comfort zones. Think of it as training for the Olympics. Sitting on the couch watching TV would be easier than running and lifting weights, but to get to the gold, an athlete has to get up off the couch and go for it. Also, let your students know that you'll be supporting them 100 percent the entire time; you're the Olympic trainer. Get the class enrolled in supporting one another as members of the team, too.

Think again about the first time you realized the training wheels were gone from your two-wheeler, it was scary, but once you recognized you were doing it anyway . . . WHEEEE!

e BELONGING

With few exceptions, students want to belong. By building their sense of belonging, you bring cohesion to the classroom atmosphere and actually speed up both your teaching and their learning.

When we look at top-performing teams, there's one thing every player shares: a sense of belonging. This belonging makes players feel they're adding value, they're contributing. They feel empowered and experience a feeling of acceptance of "me as me." When a teacher builds that belonging, she also removes threats, allows for students' brains to relax, their emotions to engage and learning to soar. This creates a feeling of team, unity, agreement and support in learning. It also accelerates the teaching process and increases learner ownership.

> *Building a sense of belonging accelerates the teaching process and increases learner ownership.*

True belonging (team cohesion) allows people to feel

empowered to step out and risk their comfort zone for success and learning. It can also create a language of support as well as standards for treating one another with respect (Singer, 1997).

Setting Traditions: Building A Sense of Belonging

As the Chicago Bulls run out onto the basketball court, the lights go out, the music blares, the spots come on, and the ritual begins: laps around the court, high-5's, whooping and chanting, the team piles-in. You'll never see the team saunter onto the court and say, "OK, let's start."

Every championship sports team starts with, ends with, and incorporates into every practice and performance, certain traditions that bring the team together and cement their success and effectiveness. You can do the same with your class to cement its great learning success and effectiveness. By doing so, you'll get students focused. Plus, the traditions satisfy all levels of the brain, livening up normally mundane tasks, and creating a team in your class.

Traditions and rituals play a significant part in our lives – from life-changing events such as funerals, weddings, marriages, graduations and birthdays – to mundane tasks like brushing our teeth. Many times traditions provide us with a sense of continuity as we travel through the passages of life. They ground us and reassure us, as well as provide us with fun and play. In setting the Quantum Teaching atmosphere, we establish traditions early in the learning to provide a sense of structure, predictability and balance, and to reduce threat and stress.

> *Traditions create a sense of shared values, agreement and belonging.*

- **Whoa Clap:** Clap in unison with upbeat music, then clap faster and faster. Pull one hand high in the air and bring the other hand to meet it, while saying "Whooooooah!" At this final clap, the music is off, learning begins.

- **Let It Go:** Like a Whoa Clap, but used to "Let it go" to break or end of period. Music starts at the final clap.

- **Clapping the Chunk:** To end a specific learning segment. You put one hand out, palm up, take the information just learned, put it in your hand and clap it closed.

- **Integrate:** Another way to bring closure. Snap your fingers three times, state an affirmation about what you just learned and pull your hands toward your chest. Snap. Snap. Snap. "I've got it!"

- **Introductions:** When a guest or new person arrives to the class or group. The class/group greets them and has a special introduction, (like everyone says one adjective that describes themselves, etc.)

Traditions create a sense of shared values and agreement. They also happen to satisfy that part of the brain which craves routine, yet in a fun, upbeat way.

We know the brain loves clean beginnings and clean endings to its learning. They help it distinguish, process and recall the experience/information in easily digestible "chunks." Too often, however, the only clean beginnings and endings to our teaching are the bells at the beginning and the end of the period. To our learner's brain, everything in between blurs into a big blob of learning/experience, even though we've taught several distinct pieces of learning during that time. When you feed the brain's cravings for clean beginnings and clean endings, it allows the brain to relax because structure and routine are there. Clean beginnings and endings can be easily built into the learning as traditions. The acknowledgments you learned earlier in this chapter will easily become traditions that students look forward to. The greatest traditions will be the ones that you and your classes create together. They'll elicit pride, team and joy in learning. Remember, the more emotional buy-in and ownership they can feel, the stronger the impact.

Remember:

Modeling builds rapport, improves credibility and enhances influence.

f MODELING

Who you are matters more than what you know. We've all heard statements such as, "Actions speak louder than words," "Walk the talk," and "Practice what you preach." These all refer to Modeling. Students often search eagerly for reasons not to buy in: holes in our story, contradictions, a mismatch of our words and actions. The more we model, however, the more they buy in and start matching us. Why do they buy in? Because they sense the congruency, the match-up between what we believe and say with what we do. As human beings, we sense when things are incongruent. Therefore, modeling is a powerful way to build rapport and relate to others. It also means less work for you but more impact on your class. Plus, it injects more energy into your teaching.

As we said earlier, everything speaks. And nothing speaks louder than actions. So consciously choose your every move.

- Model clear communication

- Acknowledge every effort

- Smile

- Use energy to create more energy

- Be a great listener

- Paraphrase their thoughts

- Step out of your comfort zone regularly and let them know that you're doing so

- Reframe or restate negative situations to find the positive in them.

Imagine . . . It's the first day of school, and as Colin leaves your classroom his heart is racing with anticipation at the thought of how learning can be. Excitement, fun and elation in a supportive, comfortable atmosphere. Where the teacher not only cares, but gets involved in his success. A smile creeps across

Colin's face, and a flood of pictures, sounds and feelings fly through his brain. He anticipates many more days like today – a year full of joy, excitement, intrigue and success.

REVIEW

As we invite students into dynamic, unforgettable, lifelong learning, we create for them a unique and powerful atmosphere in which they feel safe, yet challenged, understood and celebrated.

Take a moment to envision your students: smiling with support, seeing themselves as dynamic and successful. Hear students relating, sharing, risking and celebrating their learning. Feel the warmth of students softening their resistance as they let others share, laughing and celebrating the joy and wonder of learning.

How will you create this kind of atmosphere? See your intention for their success as it turns into the reality of their success. Hear yourself building rapport, acknowledging learning and inquiring into their wonderment. Feel the pride of sparking empowerment, joy and lifelong learning.

I Know!

Check the box if you know:

- ❏ The power of positive intention
- ❏ The role of emotions in learning
- ❏ How to build rapport
- ❏ How to tap into joy
- ❏ The impact of affirmations and acknowledgments
- ❏ The importance of celebration
- ❏ The magic of joy and wonder
- ❏ The exhilaration of risk-taking
- ❏ The warmth of belonging

Celebrate!

The exciting and nurturing atmosphere you create!

CELEBRATE

Orchestrating A Strong Foundation

CONTEXT

chapter 3

43

What if

your classroom's parameters and guidelines worked for everyone?

What if, as in a symphony orchestra, everyone in your classes knew their parts and played together in harmony?

Imagine . . . Colin breathes a sigh of relief as he plops comfortably into his chair. He loves being able to breathe easily in this class, as he always knows where he and everyone else stands. He doesn't have to sit through discipline issues or power struggles in

this class, because the foundation is firm, the guidelines clear – and everyone is playing by the same rules. Aaaah. He appreciates the clarity with which this teacher communicates as well as her consistency and fairness. Colin thinks to himself how cool it is that he and his classmates have a common vocabulary for success in their lives and in school.

Envision a set of guidelines that reach beyond the classroom, guiding behavior, building character, and teaching values that stick with the students for the rest of their lives. Imagine preparing students for the world by giving them the tools they need to make responsible decisions, and ultimately become better citizens. These benefits come from a strong foundation.

Like atmosphere, a strong foundation serves as an essential part of the learning community.

LABEL

Although the particulars of each foundation are as unique and individual as each school and class, the basic elements remain the same:

- a shared purpose,
- shared principles and values,
- powerful beliefs about learning and teaching, and
- clear agreements, policies, procedures and rules.

a PURPOSE

A learning community shares more than a common location; it also shares a common purpose. Think of the bond that cements certain communities: the medical community, the teaching community, a group of concerned neighbors. The shared interest of these people unifies them and spurs them to action. In the classroom, the shared purpose is for all students to develop proficiency in a subject, become better learners and interact as team players, in addition to developing other skills you deem important. It's up to you to determine the purpose of your community.

Once you've decided on that purpose, communicate it clearly to the students early in the school year. Make an announcement: "By the end of this year, everyone here will speak Spanish well enough to carry on a lengthy conversation." Build excitement around the purpose. Transmit it with passion and assurance. Give your students feedback often regarding their progress. Be their coach, and provide them with information about their progress and how they're playing the game. Surprise them with celebrations along the way. Keep the momentum going!

> *Shared Purpose: Students develop subject proficiency*

b PRINCIPLES

Your community's shared principles make a statement about how you collectively choose to live your lives. They're like a collective conscience. They guide behavior and help establish a trusting, supportive environment. For the principles to stick, everyone in your classroom must agree they're important and hold them in high esteem.

> *"One of the hallmarks of the learning community is a system of principles that are shared and commonly understood among the members in the organization."*
> — *Mary Driscoll, 1994*

When you teach principles, you're really teaching character. During the golden age of Greece, citizens considered character development one of the most important parts of a young person's education. Ethos, or ethic, refers to character – the way you show up in your attitudes and interactions with others. According to the Greek way of thinking, everything you do – conversations, interactions with strangers, family and friends – reveals your true character. Again, everything speaks. Think of it as living in a fish bowl where everyone can clearly see you. It's hard to appear as anything other than your true character. If honesty, persistence and dependability are part of your character, others will recognize those qualities in you and you'll be more successful in the world.

In Quantum Teaching, we use a set of principles we call the 8 Keys of Excellence. We've used these Keys in schools, businesses and our SuperCamp programs with great success. They provide a meaningful way to gain alignment and cooperation. The Keys lay the framework for a supportive, trusting environment where each person is valued and respected. Because we know that an absence of threat is one of the necessary conditions for learning to take place (Hart, 1983).

Remember:

When students feel secure, they let themselves risk more and learn more.

INTEGRITY

FAILURE LEADS TO SUCCESS

SPEAK WITH GOOD PURPOSE

THIS IS IT

COMMITMENT

OWNERSHIP

FLEXIBILITY

BALANCE

Integrity: Conduct yourself with authenticity, sincerity and wholeness. Your values and behavior are aligned.

Failure Leads to Success: Understand that failures simply provide you with the information you need to succeed. There are no failures, only outcomes and feedback. Everything can be useful if you know how to find the gift.

Speak with Good Purpose: Speak in a positive sense, and be responsible for honest and direct communication. Avoid gossip and harmful communication.

This is it: Focus your attention on the present moment, and make the most of it. Give each task your best effort.

Commitment: Follow through on your promises and obligations; live your vision. Do whatever it takes to get the job done.

Ownership: Take responsibility and be accountable for your actions.

Flexibility: Be open to change or a new approach when it helps you get the outcome you desire.

Balance: Keep your mind, body and spirit in alignment. Spend time developing and maintaining these three areas.

Carole Allen, a SuperCamp facilitator and a teacher at M.E.A.D. Creative Learning Center, an alternative school for at-risk youth near Spokane, Washington, has incorporated the Keys into nearly every aspect of her classroom. In fact, 17 teachers at M.E.A.D. have now adopted them. Allen says to make the Keys work, you must incorporate them into the lesson plan every day. "It's not enough to simply hang them on the wall and refer to them occasionally; they must be tied into the curriculum." Finding a way to bring them into nearly every lesson has helped her make the 8 Keys the foundation of her classroom, her learning community.

In the Thornton Township High Schools on the south side of Chicago, the Keys form the foundation of a district-wide Quantum Learning program. Posted on walls and woven through the lessons and games, the Keys become part of the common vocabulary between teachers and students.

As students implement the 8 Keys, behavior problems diminish – even with some challenging students. One reason for this success is, when you integrate the Keys, you focus on appropriate behavior. In most cases, teachers only refer to rules when someone breaks them. When you teach the Keys, you point out things that students do right. The 8 Keys are the guiding principles to which learners align their behavior. These principles become acceptable ways of thinking and acting. It's easy to catch students being flexible, committed or speaking with good purpose.

Catch your students using the Keys. Be on the lookout for opportunities to praise their behavior. You might say, *"I noticed you picked up the puzzles even though you weren't playing with them. Good job taking ownership for cleaning up the classroom."* Or with the older students: *"I've noticed you've really made an effort to clean up your language. I appreciate your speaking with good purpose in our class."*

When students misbehave, you can get them back on track just by mentioning the Keys. Ask open-ended questions like, *"What Key is challenging you right now? What Key could you be paying more attention to?"* This challenges the student to identify the problem and the solution, and saves you from delivering a lecture on behavior.

Teachers who use the Keys hope to get students to the

> "The Eight Keys have helped me improve my relationship with both teens and teachers. When I applied these keys to my life they helped mold my character in ways that will make me a success in life.

Leroy Hopson
Student, Thornton Township High School
Harvey, Illinois

> "Speak with Good Purpose is important to the speaker and the listener. When you use this key you say what you mean and mean what you say. How much respect you have for yourself and the person you're talking to is reflected upon using this key.

Shereeta Glasper
Student, Thornton Township High School
Harvey, Illinois

"automatic level." At that point, the Keys have become part of their lives. "First the keys become part of their language, then they become part of their behavior," Allen says. "At the automatic level, they see the world through the Keys.

"The critical piece is this: while we're with our students, we hook the Keys to all content. That's the magic. The Keys become our life. When the students are not with us, they begin to live by the set of Keys we have agreed upon as teachers and students. They're learning some things families aren't able to teach today – about life and how to survive."

Teaching the Keys

Of course, the students aren't going to follow the Keys if the teacher doesn't do the same. As Ralph Waldo Emerson once said, "What you are shouts at me so loudly, I can't hear a word you say." So the first step to teaching the Keys is modeling. Be a model of the behavior you want to see in the students. Show them the Keys through your actions. A living, breathing demonstration is more powerful than words.

Second, introduce the Keys through stories and metaphors. Stories from your own life work best. Because they have more meaning to you, they become more powerful to the students. Students yearn to know more about you; they want to hear your story. You might explain the meaning of Failure Leads to Success by sharing a time in your own life when you failed at something, but learned from the experience and used that information to succeed. Literature, fables, and even news events can also provide stories about the Keys.

Finally, work the Keys into the curriculum.

In her elementary classes, Allen had students choose a different Key each day, write it down and tape it to their desk. They would also write their name and the Key on every piece of paper they used that day. This way, the Key always sat in front of them. Another method is to write down all the Keys on slips of paper and put them in a jar. As students walk into class, they

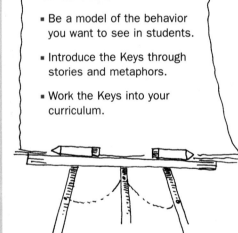

TEACHING THE 8 KEYS OF EXCELLENCE

- Be a model of the behavior you want to see in students.

- Introduce the Keys through stories and metaphors.

- Work the Keys into your curriculum.

reach into the jar and pull out a Key at random. That Key becomes their focus for the day.

To integrate the Keys over a semester course, you can spend the first two weeks giving an overview of the Keys in general. Then, take two weeks for each Key, making it the focus or backdrop for all that is taught and experienced during the month. Spend the final two weeks bringing all 8 Keys together again. For a year-long course, each key would be one month instead of two weeks.

Allen asks students to choose a school faculty member and observe that person. "Sometimes we'd do the principal, sometimes the assistant principal, sometimes the music teacher," Allen says. "I'd tell the students, 'Check her out; see if she's living in the Keys.' They'd come running back. 'Boy, she didn't live in the Keys.' 'What did she violate?' When they'd tell me, we would discuss what we could do about it, such as maybe give her the information."

At the higher grade levels, the Keys can be integrated into the lesson plan, from literature to history to science. In literature, you might ask the class "How did the main character violate or live in Integrity? Did she use Flexibility? Which keys did she exercise?"

Apply this method to other courses. Use the Keys to analyze events and raise questions and issues. History presents a wealth of opportunities for studying the Keys. For nearly any historical event or figure, you can ask your students, "What happened here? What Keys showed up? How did this affect the outcome? Which Keys does this person live by?" The same goes for current events. Even science and math courses can teach the Keys. If you're studying ecology, talk about pollution and taking ownership of the environment. In math, talk about some of the people behind the theories and the Keys by which they lived. Make the lessons personal to the students by showing them how they can apply the Keys more effectively in their own lives. Be creative; every lesson presents an opportunity to reinforce the Keys.

Dexter, an 18-year old senior, repeating a freshmen English class thought the 8 Keys, woven into the curriculum were 'stupid'.

One Monday morning, Dexter came into class early, asking to see me privately in the hallway. Having never heard Dexter initiate communication before, I enthusiastically obliged. Dexter leaned up against the lockers, looking seriously at the floor. I did the same next to him, and asked, "What's going on, Dex?" He said, "You know those keys you're always talking about?" "Sure, what about them," I replied.

"Well, I always thought they were stupid, but now I know they're not at all — they really mean something important — especially that 'Speak with Good Purpose' one.

"Well, I had this little cousin, Doo-wah. He was a punk and always in trouble — stealing things, running away. He had an attitude and no one ever had anything good to say about him or to him. People always told him that he was no good and he'd never be anything else. So he started to believe it. He joined a gang and was in and out of juvie all the time. I was the only one he really trusted and the only one who ever said anything nice to him. On Saturday he came over to my house and was worse than I had ever seen him. He said that he wanted to kill himself. I tried to cheer him up and tell him that he had options. It seemed to help but it made me mad that no one else even tried to help him.

"After he left my house that Saturday he was shot and killed. At the funeral everyone had something nice to say about him — all kinds of positive things about what the future could've been and how much potential he had. They all spoke without good purpose to him his whole life. I think that's why he's dead now. If they had spoken with good purpose earlier, it could've made a difference in Doo-wah's life."

Dexter finished saying, "Now I really get the meaning of the Keys — they do matter!"
— Sarah Singer-Nourie

C BELIEFS ABOUT LEARNERS, LEARNING AND TEACHING

Your beliefs influence your actions and behaviors. When you carry positive, affirming beliefs, they affect those around you. As Henry Ford said, "Whether you think you can or think you can't, you're right." No matter how many teaching courses you take, or how many new skills and methods you learn, your ability to reach your students remains directly proportional to your belief in yourself.

Remember:

Believe in your ability to teach and your students' ability to learn, and amazing things happen.

For some, believing in themselves comes easier than for others. The little voice in your head may keep whispering, "I'm not that good. This isn't going to work." But no matter how many times you heard it, you don't have to listen to it.

Instead, act "as if." Sometimes just acting "as if" fools our subconscious mind into believing we have current abilities beyond what we think we have, and this propels us to accomplish more.

Maybe you don't think Quantum Teaching can work. It may do the trick for someone else's class – a group of advanced, easy-to-teach students that are eager to learn – but it won't work for your group. Try it anyway. Act "as if" you know it will work. Implement the Keys and teaching methods you learn in this book. Act "as if" you're the greatest teacher in the world. Carry yourself confidently, and pretend you know exactly what you're doing. Eventually, you'll start seeing results, things will turn around, and you'll come to believe in your own abilities and those of your students.

Educator Lynn Freeman Dhority, recipient of Harvard University's Boylston Prize for Outstanding Teaching, was once afraid of trying out new, playful teaching methods with his adult students. *"As soon as I became willing to begin abandoning my fears, my playful, intuitive and spontaneous resources emerged more freely, and the same types of behavior began to occur in my students. If I am believable and fully present in my invitation to join an imaginative, playful communication, students feel freer to risk their own first steps in response."*

This approach works for students as well. For many low-achieving and learning-disabled students, low self-esteem is at the root of the problem. Far too often, negative school experiences have undermined their self-confidence and natural love of learning. They adopt the mantra, "I have a learning disability. I can't learn" or "I'm a bad speller and I hate math" "English is dumb, why even try?" In their minds, they see school as difficult, the teacher as the enemy, and they feel doomed to failure.

If you have a student who doesn't believe he can excel, suggest that he act as if he were an excellent student. Teach him to do the things excellent students do: sit in the front row, raise his hand enthusiastically, talk to the teacher, nod his head and lean forward in his seat, as if he were hanging on your every word. Together, observe other students and point out how they review their notes before class, get to class on time and ask questions when they need clarification. It may take time, but the more good habits your struggling student adopts, the better his chances for success. As he begins to feel more successful and to identify with the successful students, his self-esteem will rise – and so will his grades.

DEMONSTRATE

So start your entire class out on the right note every day. Begin the morning with Opening Questions. These questions invite positive statements your whole class will soon learn to repeat, though expect it to take a few weeks.

Make up your own Opening Questions and practice them in front of the mirror. Note how you carry yourself. Stand up straight, plant your feet firmly and use big gestures. Then try out your questions on your class.

One of the best things you can do for your students is to believe in them. Leroy Hopson, the student we quoted previously, was struggling in his Essentials class. But his teacher's belief in his abilities turned him around.

EXAMPLE OF OPENING QUESTIONS CAROLE ALLEN USES:

Teacher: Are you smart?
Students: We're smart!
Teacher: How smart?
Students: Very smart!
Teacher: How do you treat your teacher?
Students: With respect!
Teacher: How do you treat yourselves?
Students: With respect!
Teacher: What are you willing to give today?
Students: 100 percent!
Teacher: Where do you go from here?
Students: College!
Teacher: Which college?
Students: The best college!

"The most important thing was that she believed in me and gave me something to look forward to. And when the year was over, I'm proud to say I made it out of Essentials. And I know she was proud because she gave me a big hug and told me she believed I could do it all the time and that sealed our friendship forever. I got straight A's and B's. We had long talks about things I could do to improve myself, she made promises that she often kept and she was one of my best friends. Her class became my favorite and was never topped. The things I do now I do because of a great teacher and friend, Ms. Singer."

Internalize Quantum Teaching's beliefs. They may be unspoken, but when you believe in them, they'll show up in your actions. Begin to conduct your class from the point of view that you are a fantastic teacher with talented students, and anything is possible.

To the left are a few of the beliefs we like to post in our teacher training programs. You may want to post them in your classroom. Inspirational quotes from authors and historical figures also make good visuals. Add color to the posters so they catch the eye and lift the spirit.

AGREEMENTS, POLICIES, PROCEDURES AND RULES

The foundation of the learning community includes the agreements, policies, procedures and rules by which everyone is willing to live. These agreements keep order and guide the students' actions. They clarify what the teacher expects of the students. The entire school can establish these agreements, and they can be established within the classroom between teachers and students (Caine and Caine, 1997).

Fine distinctions exist among agreements, policies, procedures and rules. Classroom **agreements** are more informal than rules. They list simple, concrete ways to make things run smoother, such as listening quietly and attentively while another person is talking. Students have the right to learn. The teacher has the right to teach. No one has the right to interfere with learning or teaching. They can also include a more comprehensive agreement, such as following the 8 Keys.

Policies support the purpose of your learning community. They also explain the sequences of actions for certain situations. For example, when students are absent, it is their responsibility to get missed assignments from the teacher. Students will have the same number of days to complete their makeup work as days they were absent (i.e. gone one day, one day to make it up upon return).

Procedures let students know what to expect and what action to take. Your classroom procedure might include lining up inside the door before recess, where to place homework, how to organize the room for group work, or using the first five minutes of class time to review the previous day's learning. Familiar procedures create routine, which is important to students, not only in the lower grades, but also within all learning communities. It gives them a sense of stability, control and structure.

Rules are stricter than agreements or policies. Breaking a rule evokes clear consequences. For example, Because we support one another, there are no put-downs. If you use a put-down, you must clean it up with a 4-Part Apology. Be respectful of others by staying quiet during individual work time.

Consequences might be:

- First Violation – Warning
- Second Violation – Time Out
- Third Violation –
  Behavior Conference
  (depending on student's age)

Agreements, policies, procedures and rules fulfill the brain's need for purposeful, positive structure. Fear causes the brain to shut down. It makes students act out of basic instincts. Students feel more secure when they know the parameters, know what to expect, and have some grounding in solid agreements, policies, procedures and rules. Guidelines provide

---

A Behavior Conference is one possible consequence for rule violations. Here, the student and you meet during neutral time – outside of class time (after or before school, during a study hall), to discuss the issue at hand and find a solution together. This sample form can guide the process along. It can be filled out by the student at the beginning of and during the conference, to help the student gain clarity on the situation and work toward solving the problem. It can also help as a reference in future student-teacher communications, to remind and to redirect behavior.

SAMPLE CONTRACT – BEHAVIOR CONFERENCE

Student Name: _____

Teacher Name: _____

Date: _____

- Do you know why you got this (detention, time-out, etc.) and why we are having this conference?
- How do you feel about this situation?
- What can I do to help you get this situation under control?
- What can you do to get control of the situation before your parents or the principal becomes involved?
- Do you know what happens next if you can't solve this problem?
- Specifically, what behaviors will I expect to observe from you in the future?

Student Signature: _____

Comments / Observations

Adapted from William Glasser by Marilyn Ragland, Strategies for Learning Program, Thornton Township High Schools.

DEFINING A CLASSROOM'S PURPOSE, AGREEMENTS, POLICIES, PROCEDURES AND RULES

Step I – Developing the Rules and Consequences

■ Have a class meeting to discuss rules.

■ Pass out a single index card to each person and have them record three rules that everyone should follow.

■ List rules from the cards on the board.
  • Ask students to eliminate unnecessary ones.
  • Ask students to prioritize rules.
  • Consolidate where appropriate.

■ Once a final list is determined, get a verbal agreement from each student in support of the rules. Arrange private conferences with dissenters to find out what adjustments can be made in order for them to support it.

■ Have a second class meeting to decide the consequences of rule violations. Discuss the reasons for consequences and their feelings about them.

■ Inform students of consequences dictated by the school: detention, parent call, dean referral. However, let them know it is possible to add other deterrents that will give violators a chance to get inappropriate behavior under control.

■ Pass out index cards again and ask students to list three possible consequences.

■ List consequences from the cards on the board.
  • Ask students to eliminate unnecessary ones.
  • Consolidate where appropriate.
  • Add approved consequences to the school requirements.
  • Set a limit if necessary.

■ Once the final consequence list is determined, get a verbal okay from each student that he/she understands and approves of the consequences.

■ Duplicate and distribute copies of the rules and consequences to the students.

Adapted from William Glasser by Marilyn Ragland, Strategies for Learning Program, Thornton Township High Schools.

a secure foundation. As students stretch and grow, they need the security and feeling of support. With a secure base under them, students can more willingly step out of their comfort zones.

A solid foundation sets guidelines for action. To be effective, all the elements of the foundation must be clear to everyone. Take time to explain all policies, procedures and rules and make sure all students are in alignment and understand exactly what they mean. State all consequences clearly, and follow through. Students may assume it's all right to show up to class a few minutes late, since you never stated the agreement and they've seen no consequences for being late. You, however, may seethe inside because your students always wander in late. Clear guidelines at the outset will sidestep such misunderstandings and help your classes run smoother.

Many teachers give students a written copy of class policies and rules for the student to sign, much like a contract. This contract also lists the consequences for breaking a rule. What a great way to make sure everyone is aware of the rules and policies and committed to following them.

A final note on classroom guidelines: you'll win greater cooperation if you invite the students to help make the rules. When possible, get the students to determine the classroom policies and rules by asking them what guidelines they think are needed to support the learning community's purpose. The students take greater ownership of the rules if they help create them. By listening to their suggestions you help them feel respected and valued. The rules become the community's decision, creating greater unity.

Can you state your classroom's purpose? Your agreements, policies, procedures and rules? Are they clear to your students? If not, set aside some time to explain them, and let your students have a voice in determining new policies. You may want to use the system to the left, compiled by Marilyn Ragland, Strategies for Learning Program, Thornton Township High Schools, South Holland, Illinois.

Write down your classroom's purpose. Be sure it incorporates affective, cognitive and behavioral elements.

KEEPING THE COMMUNITY GOING (AND GROWING)

Now you know how to build the foundations of a learning community in your classroom. Keep it going!

Building a strong foundation takes time, effort and energy. It's an ongoing process. Consistent attention keeps what you've built strong and healthy. Throughout the year, be sure you continue to adhere to the guidelines you established early on. Keep supporting your classroom's purpose. Go after it with energy and zeal. Keep the students involved in the learning community and keep interest levels high. How do you do this? By treating students as partners in learning and using future pacing to pique their curiosity about what's to come.

Partners In Learning

In the past, the teacher/student model has looked something like this: the teacher, the keeper of knowledge, simply had to dump the information into the students' heads, the ready receptacles for knowledge. The teacher needed only to speak in long lectures and the students

"We learn:
10% of what we read,
20% of what we hear,
30% of what we see,
50% of what we see and hear,
70% of what we say,
90% of what we say and do."
— Dr. Vernon A Magnesen, 1983

would absorb and retain the information. The students' only job was to sit quietly at their desks and listen.

As any veteran teacher will tell you, most of the time, this just doesn't work. Studies show we retain little of the information taught us in the traditional lecture style. For real learning to take place, you must actively involve the student.

Let your students know right from the start that they are responsible for their own education. As partners in learning, they must develop and support the rules, Keys, class purpose, and all other elements that form the foundation. Help inspire and motivate them to want to learn by creating an exciting, joyful learning environment, and communicate to them that they are responsible for their outcomes.

One way to do this might be to let the students make some choices within the guidelines you set. Rather than demanding the standard oral report with notes on three-by-five cards, let students choose between the oral report, and say, creating a short skit, or even a video. Would they rather read the book first or watch the film? Solve the problem on their own or hear a hint? By giving them some options you put them in control of their education. They'll enjoy projects more, and learn more – and isn't that the point?

Future-Pacing

Future-pacing builds anticipation, WIIFM (What's In It For Me?), and partnership as you move from one lesson to another. It's the teaser you see in movie previews for next summer's release that leaves you interested and enthralled and wanting more, with just enough information to create a rough sketch of the full picture.

You can use future-pacing to build excitement about what's coming–whether it's in the next semester, the next week, or later that same day. At the beginning of this chapter, we asked you what your classroom would be like with a strong foundation. We painted a picture of a classroom with fewer discipline problems, a sense of security, strong guidelines and shared purpose. We gave you just enough information to pique your interest and leave you wanting more. That's future-pacing.

Future-pacing also means making connections. Students often complain that nothing they learn is useful in the real world. You've got to make the connection for them. Using future-pacing, creates a vision of the future for your students to share, linking future events. Even high school students some-times have trouble linking cause and effect, so spelling it out for them can be helpful. By creating a vision for students, you show them the value of what you're teaching and give them the motivation to succeed in school.

EXAMPLE OF FUTURE-PACING

At the beginning of the day when Mind Mapping will be taught and practiced . . .

"By the end of the today, you'll have the keys to unlocking your perfect memory and creative genius! You'll know what it looks like, sounds like and feels like to have more fun in any class, study less but remember more, while coloring and doodling in class!"

REVIEW

Like atmosphere, foundation builds the context for Quantum Teaching. You can create a strong founda-tion within your classroom by setting clear parameters and guidelines for students to follow. These include a shared purpose, principles, beliefs, procedures, policies, rules and agreements. These parameters must be clear to all students, and the students must commit to following them. Clear guidelines estab-lish a safe, secure classroom environment, fostering greater risk-taking and greater learning.

REVIEW

Take a moment to envision the learning community you know you want to have. Notice what your learners do, how they interact, and what they say. Feel the sense of belonging and unity. Feel the excitement as students meet each challenge, apply the 8 Keys, and enjoy increasing success.

What guidelines support this kind of learning community? See those guidelines being implemented. Know that you have the ability and the character to nurture a solid foundation for successful living.

Remember these beliefs of a Quantum Teacher . . .

- I make a difference in the world.

- Every action, thought and feeling contributes to the sum total of the planet.

- I am a free-willed being.

- The power of choice is my greatest gift.

- I am the cause of my own experience.

- I can choose how to think, feel and act. No other person makes me feel a certain way.

- Reality is personal.

- My world is different from any others.

- All students are gifted – context determines the evidence.

- People can be geniuses – create the conditions necessary.

- There are no unresourceful students, only unresourceful states.

- Change the state and behavior is changed.

- Each interaction has the capacity to heal or damage.

- Results are the sum of all healing or damages.
  All behaviors, feelings and words suggest thoughts to both the unconscious and conscious mind.

I Know!

Check the box if you know:

- ❑ The basic elements for establishing a strong foundation
- ❑ The 8 Keys of Excellence
- ❑ Three ways I plan to include them in my curriculum
- ❑ Empowering beliefs about learning and teaching

Celebrate!

Clear guidelines and agreements where everyone feels secure.

CELEBRATE

Orchestrating A Supportive Environment

CONTEXT

chapter

4

a PERIPHERALS

Iconic Content Posters

Affirmation Posters

b PROPS

c SEATING

d PLANTS, AROMA, PETS AND OTHER "ORGANIC" ELEMENTS

e MUSIC AND LEARNING

63

What if

you could teach more with less effort?

ENROLL

You can deliver more content, and have your students both understand and retain more. How? By changing your classroom environment.

EXPERIENCE

Imagine . . . As Colin nears the room, the sound of upbeat, fun music catches his attention. He starts walking to the beat of the song as he smiles and crosses the threshold. His eyes are immediately drawn to the colors, posters and welcoming bright look of the classroom. He grabs a squishy ball, one of many toys, and relaxes. From the first moment, Colin feels at home.

LABEL

We'll explore specific enhancements in a moment, but first let's get acquainted with the theory and research so that you know the *why* as well as the *what.*

All learning is dual-plane. In other words, learning happens both consciously and non-consciously at the same time. The brain is constantly flooded with stimuli, and it chooses a particular focus moment-by-moment. For example, as you read this you are consciously aware of the print, its layout and the graphics on this page. As soon as we mention temperature or the feel of the seat beneath you or the aroma in the air, your brain switches rapidly to each of these sensations. Does that mean your brain was unaware of these sensations while reading this text? Not at all. Although we consciously attend to only one input at a time, the brain is able to non-consciously attend to many things, from many sources, at once (Lozanov, 1979). That's the theory and research; now for the practical application.

The brain is constantly flooded with stimuli, and it chooses a particular focus moment-by-moment.

Take a look around your classroom. As students scan the walls of your class, what do they see? Last year's yellowed posters? A half-erased board? Faded bulletin-board paper? Misaligned stacks of papers and books? Cabinets with a depressing layer of dust? Or do they see an environment arranged and cleaned, like you would prepare your house for your guests to arrive? After all, your students are your "guests," invited for a very important event – learning.

Are the books organized neatly on the shelves? Supplies in baskets? Fresh paper on the bulletin boards? Student desks and chairs configured to best support the learning for the day? Content-related posters placed strategically for review? Affirmations in key locations? Green plants? Your classroom environment either invites and entices learners – or distracts and diverts them.

As the items in the class catch the students' eyes, what do they "say"? What associations do they bring to mind? In a class where the teacher pays little attention to the room's excellence, the message might be, "Learning is old, tired and worn-out."

On the other hand, an environment crafted to support learning might say, "Learning is fresh, alive, full of vigor," or "Come and explore!" What is your classroom environment saying? From the way posters are attached to the wall to the seating arrangement to the display of supplies to the level of cleanliness – everything speaks. Everything in the classroom environment sends a message that either propels or detracts from learning (Dhority, 1991).

Remember:
Everything speaks;
everything, always!

Let's get a better feel for a Quantum Teaching environment, one that propels learning and increases student retention.

a PERIPHERALS

A picture is worth *more* than a thousand words. When you use a visual in a learning situation, something fascinating happens. Not only does it strengthen the initial learning by stimulating the visual modality, it literally ignites the neural pathways like fireworks on a Fourth of July night. A myriad of associations are suddenly launched into consciousness. These connections provide a rich context for new learning.

How do we create and strengthen these neural pathways? Consider these two elements: peripheral vision, and the eye-brain connection.

Special Bulletin:
Peripheral vision aids in retention!

Our eyes have a wide range of perception. Try this little experiment: Place both your index fingers parallel to one another at arms length in front of you. Now, while gazing straight ahead, move your arms slowly apart. Stop when you can no longer see your fingers from the corners of your eyes. Notice the distance between your two fingers. You can "see" everything within that distance. This is known as peripheral vision and is a powerful non-conscious learning tool, especially since learning happens both consciously *and* non-consciously.

Your brain speaks to itself through associative images. This intra-brain communication is characterized by metaphoric-symbolic language. Have you ever noticed how you can think more than one thought at a time? And each thought seems to be surrounded by a plethora

Understanding the connection between peripheral vision and the brain is essential to orchestrating a supportive learning environment.

of associations? This ability is possible because of the metaphoric-symbolic nature of the brain.

So what can we do to speak the brain's language? Before we answer that question, let's take a brief look at the eye-brain connection.

Since the 1970's we've known that the movement of the eyes during learning and thinking is tied to visual, auditory and kinesthetic modalities. In other words, our eyes move according to how the brain is accessing information (Dilts, 1983). As a general rule, when our eyes move up we're either creating or recalling pictures. For example, ask someone where they parked their car and you'll notice their eyes move up as they think – as if the car is parked up in space! But is the car parked near that cumulus cloud? Of course not. We store and create visual images in our heads. Thus the person's eyes move to the location of stored or created information.

Ask someone to sing a song in their head or recall a conversation they recently had with a friend, and you'll notice their eyes moving to one or both sides. Since auditory information enters through the ears, the eyes move to that location, remembering or creating a sound, song, phrase, conversation, etc.

Feelings are stored in our bodies. When we experience confidence, success or accomplishment we often hold our heads up, straighten our shoulders and walk with purpose. When people are asked about a successful moment, their eyes look up to locate the image as they straighten their shoulders.

You'll find it easy to tap into your students' ability to non-consciously absorb information via the brain-eye partnership. Here are some ideas you can use:

Iconic Posters

Create an icon or symbol for each major concept you're teaching and draw it on a piece of paper 11" x 17" or larger. Display these iconic posters at the front of the class above eye level, providing a big picture, a global overview of the material. To view these "concepts in disguise," learners must look up. This will assist in the visual creation, storage and retrieval of the information. Leave the posters in this location until the unit of study is completed. Then, move them to a different wall to make room for the next unit's posters. Keeping the previous unit's icons visible serves as a conscious and non-conscious reminder of the information to date. If you want students to remember the content, make it easy by putting it up so they can access their visual memory every time they see it.

As your learners become accustomed to the main concepts in pictorial form, have them create the posters for upcoming units.

You may want to take this one step further and use iconic posters to preview "coming attractions." Place the next unit's iconic posters on the right wall, the location of future material. When material is exposed in this manner it creates a sense of intrigue: "I wonder what *that* poster is all about?"

Affirmation Posters

Create (or better yet have the students create) affirming motivational posters with messages like, "I can learn this!" and "I'm getting smarter with every new challenge." Place them at the sides of the room at eye level for someone who is seated. Notice that these posters are also at ear level. As students glance around the room, they "speak" these affirmative sayings as internal dialogue, thus strengthening their beliefs about learning and about the content you teach.

Color

Picture an apple in your mind. Close your eyes if it helps. Did you see it in black and white or color? Nearly everyone sees the apple in color. Why? Because the brain thinks in color. Use color to strengthen your teaching and your students' learning! Use green, blue, purple, and red for important words, orange and yellow for highlighting, and black and brown for connecting words such as "the", "and", "a", "of", etc.

Make a list of affirmations and props appropriate for your class.

b PROPS

A prop is any object that can visibly represent an idea. Some examples:

- Dolls and puppets to represent the characters in a literary work.

- A large plastic light bulb to signal the start of a brain-storming session, or the highlighting of a "bright idea."

- An arrow to visually represent "the point" you are making.

- A large pair of glasses to show the taking of a different perspective.

- A "Sherlock Holmes" hat to signify deductive reasoning.

Props not only aid visual learning, they can also assist the kinesthetic modality. Students who are highly kinesthetic can hold the prop, and get a better "feel" for the idea you're trying to convey.

c SEATING

How you configure the seating plays an important role in the orchestration of learning. In most classroom situations student desks can be arranged to support the learning objec-

tives for any given lesson. Feel free to have students rearrange their desks to facilitate the type of inter-action needed. For student presentations, teacher lectures, videos, etc., arrange the desks so that students are facing forward to help them stay focused at the front. For group work, students' desks are turned to face one another. What you're trying to achieve is flexibility.

Explore these options:

- Use a semi-circle for a large group discussion led by a facilitator who is writing the ideas on a flip-chart, white-board or chalkboard.

- Place all desks against the walls when you want to allow for individual tasks and leave the center of the room open for small group instruction or large group discussion with everyone on the floor.

- If you can, replace the traditional student desks with six-foot folding tables and folding chairs to provide for greater flexibility.

Fixed seating situations present a bit of a challenge. But though the seats are fixed, the learners are not! Have them turn sideways for small group interactions, or sit on the floor in the aisles, or at the back, sides or front of the room.

Remember:

Whether you're teaching in a fixed or non-fixed seating situation, you orchestrate the environment to maximize the moment of learning for your students.

d PLANTS, AROMA, PETS, AND OTHER ORGANIC ELEMENTS

Plants

When you think of plants, what associations come to mind? Do you think of greenery, life, growth, flowering, branching? Biology and botany teach us that plants supply our air with oxygen – and the brain thrives on oxygen. The more oxygen it gets the better it functions. Use defenbachias to enrich the oxygen supply in your classroom. Silk plants give a nice visual effect and don't require a green thumb. But they don't produce oxygen either. Since they do add to the aesthetics however, they work best in rooms with little or no natural light.

Aroma

Ah! The sweet smell of success! What does smell have to do with it? A lot! The connection between olfactory glands and the autonomic nervous system is quite strong. What we smell triggers responses such as anxiety, hunger, calmness, depression and sexuality. Often, holidays are marked by certain smells, as are places: the hospital, the locker room, the beach.

People can increase their ability to think creatively as much as 30% when exposed to certain floral odors (Hirsch, 1993). No wonder! The olfactory regions are receptors for endorphins which signal the body's response to feelings of pleasure and well-being.

What does this mean for your classroom? A little spray of the following scents increases mental alertness: peppermint, basil, lemon, cinnamon, and rosemary. Lavender, chamomile, orange and rose induce calmness and relaxation (Lavabre, 1990).

> " When I walked in, there were bright colors everywhere, different words on the walls, music all the time. It was nice — it relaxed my mind and got me focused on what I had to do that day. "
>
> Jermaine Hampton
> Student, Thorton Township High School
> Harvey, Illinois

Pets

What happens when students meet a puppy, kitten, gerbil or hamster? "Oooo. Ahhh! Can I hold it?" Very few things bring out the caring nature of students and calm them like pets do. Plus, people have strong emotional attachments to their pets. Hampshire College in Massachusetts even encourages freshmen to bring their pets with them to ease the sometimes stressful transition to college life.

Elementary teachers know a classroom pet creates opportunities to practice responsibility, nutrition, health and caring.

e MUSIC

Music has an effect on both teacher and learners. As a teacher, you can use music to set the mood, change your students' mental states and support your learning environment. Music helps learners perform better and remember more. It stimulates, rejuvenates and strengthens learning, both consciously and unconsciously. And besides, most students just love it.

You might be asking, "Why music? I have enough to think about already." The rhythm, beat and harmony of music affects the human physiology – primarily brain waves and heartbeat – in addition to evoking emotions and memories (Lozanov, 1979). Music can help bring students into an optimal learning state. Music also enables you to build rapport with students because through it, you can "speak their language."

Baroque is best

Music has a powerful effect on the learning environment. Research shows that learning is easier and quicker when the learner is in a relaxed, receptive state. The heartbeat of a relaxed individual is 60 to 80 beats per minute. Much of baroque music closely matches the relaxed heartbeat of a human being in an optimal learning condition (Schuster and Gritton, 1986). Woodwinds and violins have a lighter tone, which adds lightness and attentiveness to the learner's mood.

The playing of Mozart. coordinates breathing, cardio-vascular rhythms and brain-wave rhythm . . . . It acts on the unconscious, stimulating receptivity and perception.

Research substantiates the use of Baroque (Bach, Corelli, Tartini, Vivaldi, Handel, Pachelbel, Mozart) and classical (Satie, Rachmaninoff) music to stimulate and maintain an optimal learning environment. Baroque's melodic chord structures and instrumentation assist the body in accessing an alert yet relaxed state (Schuster and Gritton, 1986).

Then there's the "Mozart Effect." Researchers have found that students who listen to Mozart's music seem to retain information more readily and get higher test scores. "Listening to such music (Mozart's piano music) may stimulate neural pathways important to cognition," reports University of California at Irvine researcher Dr. Frances H. Rauscher (Brown, 1993). According to French researcher, Mme. Belanger, "The playing of Mozart coordinates breathing, cardiovascular rhythms and brain-wave rhythm.... It acts on the unconscious, stimulating receptivity and perception" (Rose, 1987, p. 98).

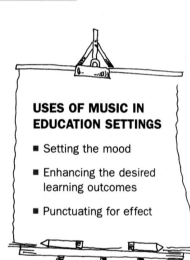

USES OF MUSIC IN EDUCATION SETTINGS

■ Setting the mood

■ Enhancing the desired learning outcomes

■ Punctuating for effect

Mix your Baroque selections with classical music to add variety in tempo, rhythm, and dynamics. Notice that upper register instruments (flutes, violins) bring a lighter tone which you may find useful during early morning and afternoon learning. To relax students after stressful situations, experiment with the sounds of piano, cellos and violas. Music also helps to mask "white noise" (the hum of lights, voices in an adjacent room, etc.) and creates a sustained supportive ambiance. Set the music's volume at a level that's just perceptible when there is silence in the room.

What music do you listen to when you're in a great mood? Is it different from the music you listen to when you're feeling nostalgic, sorrowful or romantic? Most people select music that enhances their present state of mind.

Music can also help to shift states of mind. When you've had a particularly challenging day and your next event is an evening of dancing, you can play music when you get home that soothes the transition in your mind from work to play. These same effects can work in your classroom to support the learning outcomes you're trying to achieve.

Music can be used a variety of ways in an educational setting. For starters, let's focus on these three:

- Setting the mood
- Enhancing the desired learning outcomes
- Punctuating for effect

Setting the Mood

Imagine this: Your students are pouring in from the hallway after spending an hour in a less-than-interesting previous class. How about helping them shift states by playing an upbeat, positive, contemporary selection as they arrive? You'll get their attention and at the same time suggest their time in your classroom will be light, positive and active. Hearing upbeat contemporary music between learning sessions stimulates the body toward movement and changes not only your learners' mental state, but yours also, thus allowing everyone to literally switch gears. Points to consider when selecting your music:

- Choose from a variety of contemporary artists
- Select music with a positive message.

As the pace and mood of learning changes, like when it's time for them to journal or write an essay, switch the music to a slower, instrumental selection to induce a state of reflection. When they're studying, reading or preparing notes, Mind Maps and other graphic organizers, use Baroque music to increase focus.

Enhancing Desired Learning Outcomes

The music you play can also assist you in facilitating movement and regulating the volume of sound in the room. Let's say you're about to ask your students to

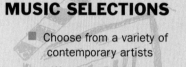

MUSIC SELECTIONS

- Choose from a variety of contemporary artists
- Select music with a positive message.

hot tip

During classes, workshops and seminars, cue your participants as to when to begin the session and return from break by playing a particular upbeat selection. Choose a song familiar to everyone, has lyrics, and is full of energy.

Rather than taking your time, energy and voice to get everyone's attention, let the music do it for you.

spend a few moments talking to one another regarding the material learned so far in this lesson. When they begin sharing, play the music as loud as their voices. Without the music, students often hesitate, wondering who will speak first and not wanting to be the first to "break the ice." The music helps them feel free to talk, to "go for it" without drawing attention to themselves. After a few moments, turn the music down a bit. Their voices will drop to match the music's volume. When it's time to get their attention, simply turn the music up so it's obviously louder and then lower it to zero. This creates a dead space which causes many students to look to find out what happened to the music. This way, rather than taking your time, energy and voice to get everyone's attention, you're using the music to do it for you. As for what type of music to play during group activities, we suggest reggae with few or no words, new age and instrumental contemporary jazz.

As students transition from group assignments to individual tasks or vice versa, go back to the upbeat music to set a tone of movement, prompting students to get up and move quickly.

In general, all musical selections will be instrumentals. Only music for breaks and certain special effects will contain lyrics. And when you do use music with lyrics, remember to choose lyrics with positive messages.

Punctuating for Effect

Sound effects help create an environment of play, interest, and entertainment, and can punctuate a main idea. When you want to signal that you're about to make an important point, you can have a phone ring and say, "Oh, this must be for you!" Recorded applause can enhance the students' applause after a solo or group presentation. Game show theme songs can add to the feeling of play and suspense. Play the "Jeopardy" theme while a team of learners prepares to give an answer. A steam-engine locomotive sound could be used with the statement "I think I can, I think I can" while students are attempting to solve a new equation or formula. Old radio show recordings provide a wealth of ideas for the use of sound effects. Explore the use of sound effects to enhance interest and attentiveness in your classroom.

It may take a while for you to learn how to weave music artfully into your classroom environment. So go ahead and experiment. Discover how you can:

- energize
- stimulate experiences
- induce relaxation
- increase focus
- develop rapport
- set a theme for the day
- inspire
- have fun

UTILIZE MUSIC TO:

- energize
- stimulate experiences
- induce relaxation
- increase focus
- develop rapport
- set a theme for the day
- inspire
- have fun

Specific Music Suggestions

Studying, Reading, Learning, Presenting:

- *Mozart Flute Concertos*
- *Relax With The Classics: Andante and Pastorale*
- *Six Duets for Two Flutes*
- The Pachelbel Canon in D
- *The Instruments of Classical Music, Volume One*

Special Music for fun:

- *TV's Greatest Hits* Series
- Disney's *For Our Children*

Break Music:

- Movie Soundtracks
- Hit Collections from the 60s, 70s, 80s, 90s
- Contemporary Jazz

- Ethnic/Cultural:
  - African Drums
  - Irish/Celtic Dance
  - Spanish Flamenco

Music for Reflection:
- Windham Hill Records: *A Winter's Solstice*
- Yanni: *Out of Silence*
- Ray Lynch: *Deep Breakfast*

REVIEW

REVIEW

Your classroom environment impacts students' ability to focus and retain information. Such enhancements as iconic posters visually display your content while affirmation posters strengthen students' internal dialog. Props bring abstract ideas alive and provide a way for kinesthetic learners to get their hands on it. Seating arrangements support the learning outcomes. Move the desks or tables so students can focus on the task at hand. Music unlocks optimal learning states and helps elicit associations. Baroque is best for studying, reviewing, and moments of concentration. Other styles can be used during breaks, journaling, group work and transitions. Orchestrating the elements in your environment greatly influences your ability to teach more with less effort.

I Know!

Check the box if you know how to use:

- ❏ Peripherals to reinforce beliefs and content
- ❏ Props to make content come alive
- ❏ Interactive, relaxed seating for interest
- ❏ Plants for relaxing effect
- ❏ Music to enhance state

Teaching more with less effort!

CELEBRATE

Orchestrating Dynamic Design

ENROLL

What if

your teaching and learning design closed the gap between your world and your students' quickly and naturally every time?

What if you could design lessons that captured students' learning styles, tapped into their array of intelligences, unleashed their motivation and set them up for success?

Imagine . . . *Colin leans forward, eyebrows raised, finding himself actually intrigued by what the teacher has just asked. "Would you be interested in . . . . ?" "What if you could . . . . ?" In spite of himself, Colin becomes hooked. He feels like the teacher has crawled inside his reality, found what might work, and asked the question of only him. Before he knows it, he finds himself in a full-scale game involving every student in the room. She has definitely piqued his interest.*

The students move around, interacting, being challenged and actually having fun – in class! He loves the game they play, although by the end of it, Colin finds himself with even more questions than he had before. He raises his hand. "That was cool, but what about . . . . " And . . . . BAM! The teacher asks for a drumroll, flips a page on the flip-chart, and suddenly the experience Colin just had not only makes perfect sense, but has a whole new meaning, based on what just happened. Inside Colin's head, a light bulb blinks on.

E X P E R I E N C E

a FROM THEIR WORLD TO OUR WORLD

The prime directive of Quantum Teaching lies in your ability to close the gap between our world and theirs. This enables you to strengthen rapport, accomplish material faster, make learning more permanent, and ensure transfer.

In our own interviews with kids, we learned that their top reason for not listening to or liking their teachers is, "They don't relate to me." A gap exists between our world and theirs. With this gap in place, students can't relate to us or see a WIIFM (What's In It For Me?) in our teaching. Without the WIIFM, they don't buy in. As experts on the human brain tell us, if there's no emotional engagement, there's no learning. When you understand students' interests, desires and thinking, and you let them know you understand, you enter their world, rather than teaching strictly from your point of view.

By the very design of your teaching you can cross over into their world and bring them over to yours, into the learning. As you consciously enter their world, you build a necessary partnership with them in the learning process. We work together on this "learning thing." This creates relevance for them and the process feels much more like real-life learning: I start in my *own* world, discover a question that lures me into some *other* world of learning, and bring back new learning to *my* world.

b MODALITIES V-A-K

In the previous chapter, we explored, discovered and unraveled the eye-brain connection with modalities. One way to think of a modality is as a neural network. Much more complex than a television network, each neural network has infinite possibilities, all stemming from the same place. From Chapter 4, you now know how to tell which modality a person's brain is tuned into at any moment. Now, how great would it be if you could tap into those modalities easily in your teaching – literally speak the same language as your learners' brains?

While most people have access to all three modalities – visual, auditory and kinesthetic – almost everyone has a pre-ferred learning modality (Bandler and Grinder, 1981) which acts

 Chapter 4 page 68

as a kind of filter for their learning, processing and communication. Not only do people have a preferred modality, they also have preferred combinations of modalities which afford them specific natural gifts and challenges (Markova, 1992).

Visual: This modality accesses visual images, created or remembered. Colors, spatial relationships, mental snapshots and pictures predominate in this modality. Someone highly visual might exhibit these characteristics:

- organized, observant, appearance-oriented
- memorizes by picture, would rather read than be read to
- needs overall view and purpose and a vision for the details; remembers what was seen

Auditory: This modality accesses sounds and words of all kinds – created or remembered. Music, tone, rhythm, rhyme, internal dialogue and voice predominate here. Someone highly auditory can be characterized as follows:

- easily distracted
- speaks in rhythmic pattern
- learns by listening, moves lips/says words when reading
- dialogues both internally and externally

Kinesthetic: This modality accesses motion and emotion of all kinds – created or remembered. Movement, coordination, rhythm, emotional response and physical comfort predominate here. Someone highly kinesthetic often:

- touches people and stands close, moves a lot
- learns by doing, points when reading, responds physically
- memorizes by walking and seeing

Just as we all have learning modality preferences, we also have teaching modality preferences. They usually

VISUAL

- Use flip-charts marked with colors instead of chalkboards. Then, hang the charts with key information around the room as you present it, and refer back to them later.
- Encourage students to chart out information, using mapping, diagrams and colors. Allow time for this.
- Stand still while presenting chunks of information; move around in between chunks.
- Distribute copies of key phrases or outlines of the lesson, leaving space for notes.
- Color-code materials and equipment; encourage students to organize their learning using different colors.
- Use iconic language in your presentation by creating visual symbols or icons to represent key concepts.

AUDITORY

- Use vocal variation (inflection, pace, volume) in your presentation.
- Teach the way you test: if you present information in a specific order or format, test the information in the same way.
- Use call-backs, having students repeat key concepts and directions back.
- After each chunk of teaching, have students tell their neighbor one thing they learned.
- Sing key concepts or have students create songs/raps about them.
- Develop and encourage students to come up with mnemonic devices to help them remember key concepts.
- Use music pieces as cues for routine activities (i.e. circus music for cleaning up supplies).

KINESTHETIC

- Use props as you teach to spark curiosity and add emphasis to key concepts.

- Create simulations of concepts to allow students to experience them.

- When working with students individually, give parallel assistance by sitting next to them rather than in front of or behind them.

- Try to speak to each student individually every day – even a greeting to the class as they walk in or a "Great participation today" as they leave.

- Demonstrate concepts while allowing students to perform step by step.

- Share your own personal experiences of learning insights with the class, and encourage them to do the same.

- Allow for movement in the classroom.

correspond to our learning style; if you're a mostly visual learner, you're probably a mostly visual teacher. It comes naturally to you. However, that's not the case with your students. Some may have the same learning modality as you, but there may be many who do not. Those who don't are most likely to miss out on what's being taught or have more challenges in learning material easily. They literally process the world through a different language than you do. Wouldn't you love to reach students with all the different modalities – and do it consistently?

While our learning and teaching reflect our modality preferences, research shows that the more modalities we can tap at the same time, the more vivid, meaningful and permanent the learning. Think of it as losing yourself in a good movie with Technicolor, stereo and full emotional and therefore physical engagement.

According to Richard Restak, " Each time a particular pattern of neurons 'fires,' it becomes that much easier for the same pathway to be activated again" (Restak, 1995, p. 92). In this case, by tapping more modalities during our teaching we fire more neural pathways which strengthen our students learning.

C THE SUCCESS MODEL FROM THE DESIGNER'S VIEWPOINT

Imagine students in your class confidently raising their hands to answer questions and participating regularly, instead of holding back and doubting themselves in front of their peers. Actually, you can easily orchestrate the learning so that students never have to contend with what we call "a double whammy" (stay tuned).

We propose the notion that, no matter how we orchestrate the design of the learning, we always set students up – for something. Maybe we intend to do this, maybe we don't, but the design always sets up the learning, risk, success or failure that results. As you know,

Everything Is On Purpose

so in this case, how can your lesson design ensure their success?

You see, two major factors help determine your students' success at any moment:

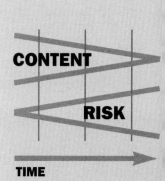

CONTENT

RISK

TIME

DIFFICULTY OF CONTENT
AND
DEGREE OF PERSONAL RISK

We know that either the difficulty of content or the degree of personal risk by themselves could be enough to make a student hold back or downshift (Jensen, 1994), bringing all learning to a screeching halt. As you know, some students consider it a huge personal risk and difficult experience to stand up or be singled out in front of the class to say or answer anything. Compound that huge personal risk with having to master hard content, and a student doesn't stand a chance for success.

Unintentionally, students are set up for a "double whammy": hard content + big risk. For example, we teach a new concept, then five seconds later ask, "Johnny, what's the answer to ____?" Johnny instantly has to contend with the hard content *and* his own personal risk of stepping out there. Yikes! Not all students have the same personal risk issues, yet we do find these factors in even the most confident adult learners. Students learn to deal with the "double whammy," but now they don't have to. The Quantum Teaching Success Model lets you set students up for success every time.

With student success as your goal, remember these elements. First, when you introduce the content (the most difficult point for a learner), make sure you ALWAYS present it in a way that is:

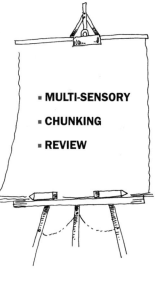

- **MULTI-SENSORY**
- **CHUNKING**
- **REVIEW**

- **multi-sensory** – use visual, auditory and kinesthetic elements

- **chunked** down – break information into chunks of three to four "infobytes" at a time, and

- contains frequent **review** – throughout learning use review to ensure the brain's storage of information. Then, add a simple progression to the learning.

As you first teach this information, make sure to make it multi-modal. Chunk it and review it frequently. Teach it first to

LARGE GROUP   SMALL GROUP   INDIVIDUAL

CONTENT

RISK

TIME

DEMONSTRATE

the large group (entire class). Then, have the small group (cooperative groups, teams or just pairs) strengthen the learning. Then finish with the individual (answering questions in front of class, homework, test or quiz). This way, learners get the information in its easiest form while taking the smallest risk in the large group. Then, as you move them to a small group, the personal risk, though greater because they're accountable one-on-one, is less pressing because they've become familiar with the content. Finally, when they perform on their own as individuals, they're still taking a big risk, but they can handle it because they feel confident, as the content is solid.

d THE QUANTUM TEACHING DESIGN FRAME

Would you like to design a scenario like the one at the beginning of this chapter? The learning can actually be that dynamic... consistently and easily. We call it:

EEL Dr. C

You probably noticed our little "Maestro" icon in the margins of Chapters 2, 3 and 4, with the words **E**nroll, **E**xperience, **L**abel, **D**emonstrate, **R**eview and **C**elebrate under it. (For ease of remembering them, we devised the non-sensical acronym "EEL Dr. C.") In Chapter 1, we explained briefly that these elements make up the Quantum Teaching Design Frame. And in fact, they form the whole structural basis upon which Quantum Teaching is built. Now we'd like to explore EEL Dr. C in more detail because, with a full understanding of it, you can design the kind of classroom scenario that began this chapter. Here we go.

Regardless of content area, grade level or audience, this frame guarantees that students become interested in and intrigued with every lesson. It also ensures that they have an experience of the learning, get practice, make the content real for themselves and anchor their success. As we explained in the opening, icons appear throughout the book to give you an idea of the flow of the frame. Obviously, a book looks different than a classroom. But they do use the same elements. The Quantum Teaching Design Frame goes like this:

Enroll	Hook them, create intrigue, satisfy WIIFM.
Experience	Give them an in-body experience of learning; create a "need to know."
Label	Drop the "data" in at the moment of peak intrigue.
Demonstrate	Provide this opportunity for them to connect experience with the new data, so they internalize it and make it personal.
Review	Cement the big picture.
Celebrate	Remember, if it's worth learning, it's worth celebrating! Celebrating anchors learning with positive association.

When applying this frame to your own teaching and lesson design, these guidelines might help:

ENROLL

Why – Enrolling establishes rapport and commonality or relate-ability. It taps into their experience, finds the "Yes!" response, and gets commitment for exploration.

Guiding Questions – To what can they relate? To what will they agree? What's in it for them (WIIFM)? To what will they commit?

Strategies – Enrolling questions, pantomime, skit, role-play, video, story.

What if we told you the punchline before the joke? Would you feel as motivated to listen? Would you get the "pop" that comes after the joke builds? NO! Yet we often do this unwittingly in our teaching.

But blowing punchlines is different from setting outcomes and context. The old paradigm of, "List all of your behavioral objectives on the board" provides the road map but does little to enroll students in the learning. Like punchlines at the beginning of jokes, outlined objectives give students a quick and easy choice. They look at those objectives within the first minute of class and make a choice – if they like them, they buy in for the class; if they don't, they check out. Many students choose to check out. We must REFRAME their experience.

Setting outcomes creates WIIFM and a framework of intrigue for the learning. Teachers can do this easily while enrolling the students and saving the punchlines at the same time! Which would you find more inviting?

a. Today we're going to read a short story about a student in Japan. *or*

b. By the end of this period, we'll have traveled to another land, met a brave, young person a lot like you, and learned how to "make it" in the face of great challenge and fear.

We hope you chose 'b'. Does it say the same thing as 'a'? Yes, but in a way that enrolls and invites, creating intrigue, anticipation and buy-in!

EXPERIENCE

Why – This provides learners with the experience, and capitalizes on the brain's natural desire to explore. Experience allows you to teach "through the back door," to tap into students' present knowledge and power of curiosity.

Guiding Questions – What is the best way for these students to "get" the information? What game or activity would tap into what they already know? What game or activity would facilitate their "need to know"?

Strategies – Use mnemonics, games and simulations. Act out elements of the new learning, role-play. Assign team tasks and activities that activate prior knowledge.

When you learn anything in real life, you initially have an experience, an engagement with the concept. Then, as the experience unfolds, you gather information which assists you in your ability to make meaning. This information takes the abstract and makes it concrete. Touching the stove and screaming "Ouch!" created a "teachable moment." You really understood "hot – don't touch." Abstract to concrete.

Experience Before Label

The experience creates emotional engagement, which we know from Chapter 2 creates an opening for meaning (Label). The experience also creates mental questions to be answered such as Why? How? What? So, the experience builds students up, creates those question marks in their minds, gets them to the edge of their seats and then . . . BAM – you label it! Instant teachable moment. Which leads us to . . .

Chapter 2 page 21

LABEL

Why – It capitalizes on the brain's natural desire to label, sequence and define. It builds on students' present knowledge and the power of curiosity. Labeling is the moment to teach the concepts, thinking skills and learning strategies.

Guiding Questions – What "distinctions" need to be made in their learning? What should you add to their understanding? What strategies, hot tips, thinking tools would be useful for them to know or use?

Strategies – Use graphic organizers, color, props, flip-charts and posters on the wall. If you used a mnemonic or metaphor, reference it here.

LABEL
"Believe it or not, this Oreo is just like a good essay – crunch in the beginning, satisfying filling in the middle, and crunch to finish it off. Otherwise known as Introduction, Body, Conclusion." The teacher pulls out a large fake Oreo with each part labeled: 'introduction, body, conclusion,' having the students name the parts as they go. Again they chant, *"It takes the crunch at the beginning, the filling in the middle and the crunch at the end!"*

Here's where we get to satisfy the students' brains – left on the edge of their seats, full of questions about the experience. Perfect! Labeling is the information, the facts, formulas, reasons, places, etc. Typically, we start here, with the content of our lesson, and then do an activity (experience) later if we have time. We now know this method is backwards if you really want to create meaning and engagement in the learning. For example, many of us learned from someone how to balance a checkbook. Yet we had to experience the frustration of attempting to balance a checkbook and not succeeding to be able to ask the right questions and get the information (label) we needed to connect with the reality of checkbook balancing. This same principle has us re-teaching information to our students. They got the information, but had to get an experience to really make the knowledge meaningful.

DEMONSTRATE
Teacher hands out one
more cookie to each stu-
dent, having them pull
them apart, and, in pairs,
label the three parts as the
parts of the essay before
eating them. Each pair of
students then gets a short
essay printed on a sheet of
paper, which they then cut
into the three parts of an
essay, drawing the corre-
sponding Oreo part on
each piece.

DEMONSTRATE

Why – It provides students the opportunity to translate and apply their new knowledge into other learning, and into their life's repertoire.

Guiding Questions – In what ways could students demonstrate their level of competency with the new knowledge? What criteria could you and they develop together to guide the quality of their demonstrations?

Strategies – Team skits, create your own video, board game, rap, song, graphic representations.

Remember learning to do something for the very first time, like riding a bike? You tried, then fell down (experience). You tried again, stopped, asked question, perhaps got some coaching from a big sister or a friend (label). Then you really made the connection by showing and doing it! When the experience and the label came together, the learning exploded into your demonstration of Wheeeeee! Down the street – cemented into your muscle memory. You needed to have that opportunity to make the learning stick. Your students need that same opportunity to make the connection, practice and show what they know.

REVIEW

Why – Review strengthens the neural connec-tions and establishes a sense of "I know I know this!" Therefore, reviewing must be done multi-modal and multi-intelligence, preferably in a different context than originally presented (game show, role play, etc.).

Guiding Questions – What is the best way for students to review this learning? In what way will each student have the opportunity to review?

Strategies – *I know I know* check-offs (like at the end of each chapter in this book); opportuni-ties for students to teach their new knowledge to others (another class, different age group, take on a new persona like teacher, expert, famous person); call-backs (you call out something like

REVIEW
The students draw
their own parts of
the Oreo essay in
their notebooks.
Before munching the
remaining cookies,
each student pulls
theirs apart, labeling
each essay part.

"Introduction, body, conclusion" and they repeat it back in unison); trio reviews (in groups of three, they walk around the room reviewing the flip chart pages to review what they learned together); Yes! Clap (putting one hand out, you put the learning in that hand, and clap it in with a loud, "Yes!")

Once you got your balance on that bike and demonstrated to everyone on the block that you could do it, you had to really make sure you had it. You still feared losing it if you stopped doing it for a while. Hence, "Practice makes permanent." Take this perfect opportunity to put the Success Model into place and let the small groups work their magic. This can be as elaborate as learning teams reviewing game-show style with one another or as simple as, "Turn to your neighbor and together review the first 10 elements on the periodic chart visually, auditorially and physically."

CELEBRATE!

Why – Celebration brings closure by honoring effort, diligence and success. Again, if it's worth learning, it's worth celebrating!

Guiding Questions – For this particular learning, what's the most appropriate way to celebrate? How can you acknowledge everyone for their accomplishments?

Strategies – high fives, team chants, show off for visitors, class party.

As you conquered staying balanced on your bike, everyone cheered, and you knew you had it. That anchored your success and gave you the motivation to try again and again. Your students' learning needs the same reinforcement. So celebrate!

To make your designing even easier, we offer the following learning planning guide. Feel free to photocopy the information for your own classroom use. Use it as you design lessons that capture students' natural desire to learn.

CELEBRATE
The pairs give high-fives to other pairs, chanting *"It takes the crunch at the beginning, the filling in the middle, and the crunch at the end."*

Class _____ Unit _____

ENROLL

How will I hook them?
What would answer
"WIIFM"?
"I'm interested."

_____
_____
_____
_____
_____
_____
_____
_____
_____

Props • Materials • Music

❏ _____
❏ _____
❏ _____
❏ _____
❏ _____
❏ _____
❏ _____
❏ _____
❏ _____

S L I M - n - B I L

EXPERIENCE

What will they DO to get it?
"I wonder what's
coming next?"

_____
_____
_____
_____
_____
_____
_____
_____
_____

Props • Materials • Music

❏ _____
❏ _____
❏ _____
❏ _____
❏ _____
❏ _____
❏ _____
❏ _____
❏ _____

S L I M - n - B I L

LABEL

What are the Ahas,
Distinctions, How-to's?
"Oh, I understand."

_____
_____
_____
_____
_____
_____
_____
_____
_____

Props • Materials • Music

❏ _____
❏ _____
❏ _____
❏ _____
❏ _____
❏ _____
❏ _____
❏ _____

S L I M - n - B I L

Lesson _____ Date _____

DEMONSTRATE

How do they get to
SHOW what
they know?

"Watch this!"

_____
_____
_____
_____
_____
_____
_____
_____

Props • Materials • Music

❑ _____
❑ _____
❑ _____
❑ _____
❑ _____
❑ _____
❑ _____
❑ _____
❑ _____

S L I M - n - B I L

REVIEW

How do students
CEMENT it in?

"I Know, I Know!"

_____
_____
_____
_____
_____
_____
_____

Props • Materials • Music

❑ _____
❑ _____
❑ _____
❑ _____
❑ _____
❑ _____
❑ _____
❑ _____
❑ _____

S L I M - n - B I L

CELEBRATE

How does every
PERSON and EFFORT get
acknowledged?

"I did it!"

_____
_____
_____
_____
_____
_____
_____

Props • Materials • Music

❑ _____
❑ _____
❑ _____
❑ _____
❑ _____
❑ _____
❑ _____
❑ _____
❑ _____

S L I M - n - B I L

HOW Are You Smart?

THE MULTIPLE INTELLIGENCES MEET SLIM-n-BIL

If we asked you who of the following was the most intelligent, what would you say: Michael Jordan, Picasso, Elie Wiesel, Albert Einstein or John Steinbeck? Tough call, yes? Could you really say that any one of them has more intelligence than the others?

For years, we've asked one big question of our students via assessment, grading and lesson design: "How smart are you?" Because of Binet, we once thought intelligence was a fixed capacity. We've measured intelligence through I.Q. tests, standardized test scores and academic cognitive performance for a long time. By design, some kids rise to the top, some fall to the bottom, and others hang in the middle – hence the trusty old bell curve.

Thanks to the brilliant work of Dr. Howard Gardner, a cognitive psychologist and co-director of Project Zero at Harvard University, we've experienced a major paradigm shift in the way we view "intelligence," from psychology to education. We've gone from, "How smart are you?" to "HOW are you smart?" This has come about through the development of Multiple Intelligences (Gardner, 1983). In his work, Gardner uncovered several different kinds of intelligence – not just one that can be measured and summed up like an I.Q. Intelligence. His theory offers a much broader view of intelligence and suggests that intelligence is a continuum that could be developed throughout life. Gardner's work has opened educators to new possibilities and challenges. We've learned new ways to facilitate deep understanding in the business of education through multiple intelligences (Gardner, 1991). So no one can answer the "Who's the most intelligent" question we posed earlier, because each one of those people is intelligent in a different way. Gardner, in fact, wrote an entire book just comparing geniuses of the different intelligences (Gardner, 1990).

To remember all of the intelligences easily, we like to think of our friends SLIM-n-BIL (a couple of cool teacher friends of ours who've mentally slimmed down a lot since they discovered the multiple intelligences. Let's check them out.

Spatial-Visual – thinking in images and pictures. This involves the ability to comprehend spatial relationships and mental images, and to accurately understand the visual world.

drawing, sketching, doodling, visualizing, images, graphics, designs, charts, art, video, movies, illustrations.

Linguistic-Verbal – thinking in words. This allows for adept use of language in speaking, writing, reading, linking and interpreting.

words, speaking, writing, storytelling, listening, books, tapes, dialogue, discussion, poems, lyrics, spelling, foreign languages, letters, e-mail, speeches, papers, essays.

Interpersonal – thinking by communicating with other people. This refers to "people skills" – being able to read, communicate and interact with other people easily.

leading, organizing, interacting, sharing, caring, talking, socializing, manipulating, mediating, group games, clubs, friends, cooperative groups.

Musical-Rhythmic – thinking in rhythms and melodies. Gardner says, "There are several roles that musically inclined individuals can assume, ranging from the avant-garde composer who attempts to create a new idiom, to the fledgling listener who is trying to make sense of nursery rhymes" (Gardner, 1983, p. 104).

singing, humming, tapping, rhythm, melody, pacing, timbre, musical instruments, rhyme.

Naturalist – thinking in reference to nature. A new arrival in Gardner's intelligences, this deals with one's affinity with nature, being able to see connections and patterns in the natural world and identify and interact with its processes.

nature-walking, animal interaction, categorizing, star-gazing, forecasting, simulations, discovery.

Bodily-Kinesthetic – thinking through physical sensations and movement. This attribute is the ability to control and use the physical body easily and deftly.

dancing, running, jumping, touching, creating, trying, simulating, assembling/disassembling, role-playing, games, tactile.

Intrapersonal – thinking reflectively. This refers to reflective awareness of one's own feelings and thought processes.

thinking, meditating, dreaming, being quiet, setting goals, reflecting, brooding, journaling, self-assessing, time alone, self-paced projects, writing, introspection.

Logical-Mathematical – thinking by reasoning. This incorporates logical, scientific problem-solving and mathematical abilities.

experimenting, questioning, calculating, deductive and inductive logic, organizing, facts, puzzles, scenarios.

As you may have already guessed, we all have different natural strengths and challenges in the multiple intelligences. As you read through them, you probably identified some of yours. We can also easily identify which school classes and activities specialize in which intelligences:

S - art, geometry, drafting

L - language arts

I - cooperative learning, group projects

M - music, choir, band

N - outdoor and environmental education

B - physical education

I - study hall, quiet time, homework, advisory

L - math, science, history

Clear? It's also clear that as students progress into higher grades, the work becomes more and more focused on two of the intelligences: Linguistic and Logical-Mathematical. Just look at the SAT test: it has always contained two parts – Verbal and Math. Great – if a student happened to be strong in those two intelligences. If not, then what? What about that artist in your class who would much rather draw than write or compute? Academically, there's a mismatch here. Plus, just as modality preferences come through in our teaching styles and lesson design, so do our intelligence preferences.

We tend to compartmentalize in our lives and our teaching, sticking with what we know and avoiding what we don't feel skilled or comfortable in. For example, if you've decided that you're not a tennis player, not a public speaker, and not a dancer, guess what activities you tend to avoid?

Unfortunately, by adulthood many of us feel so sure about this that we've tied ourselves up in "nots." The good news: Even though we have certain strengths and preferences, we can develop and strengthen other intelligences. For example, Albert Einstein claimed that he *developed* his scientific intelligence. The New City School in St. Louis has used Multiple Intelligences as the foundation for all teaching and learning (Boggeman, 1996). There, teachers found that by having students cross-train in different intelligences, receiving un-pressured, consistent experience in each intelligence, their favorites changed. *Voilá* – balance!

We can easily do this in our own teaching, too. By infusing the Multiple Intelligences into our content and teaching design, we help students automatically get more meaning and brain stimulation in their learning, offer them more variety and fun, AND stretch and strengthen their intelligences! To do this, however, we must step outside our comfort zones in our teaching and lesson design.

One way to create cross-training is through Quantum Teaching's Smart Stations – stations for the different kinds of "smart." Place actual stations around your classroom for each of the Multiple Intelligences. Students visit the stations to engage in each of the intelligences for a

DEMONSTRATE

SMART STATIONS APPLIED
You can design content-specific stations for your material. For example, to teach a novel or short story:

S – Draw a visual representation of what the story was about.

L – Write an essay.

I – With a group, act out a scene from the story and talk about how it felt.

M – Create a song or rap that tells the story.

N – Change the physical settings of the story and tell how the story would be different.

B – Create a dance or hand-jive to remember the plot sequence of the story.

I – Put yourself in the shoes of one of the characters and write a journal entry from that person's perspective.

L – Create a timeline of the story.

hot tip

In a typical unit of instruction, commit one day of the content to each intelligence. Culminate with a Smart Station integration/assessment, where students actually produce something at each station. What a great opportunity to authentically assess where ALL of the students stand with their learning!

Chapter 5
pages 94-95

specified period of time. This can occur in groups or individually, in one class period or stretched over time. They can be raw experiences of the focused intelligence, such as:

S	–	"Pictionary"
L	–	"Scattergories"
I	–	a group activity
M	–	a song or rap
N	–	an activity in nature
B	–	a dance or athletic activity
I	–	a reflection
L	–	a logic puzzle

Finally, weave SLIM-n-BIL into the design of your lessons. As you use the Design Frame on pages 94-95, tap into at least five of the intelligences. (Stay tuned for further developments as Dr. Gardner explores other kinds of intelligences. For example, 'existential', the ability to contemplate on big issues such as "Why do we exist?" As additional intelligences become substantiated, you'll want to add them to the design of your lessons as well.)

f USE OF METAPHOR, IMAGERY AND SUGGESTION

Imagine it's the first day of school, and you easily enroll students, anchor positive associations to learning, and appeal to all learning modalities. To do this you might start your class off with a story such as:

A man walked along in the hot sunlight through an unfamiliar area. He had been walking all day when he got an uncomfortable feeling in his stomach and began to worry that he might be on the wrong road. Just then he was startled to see an old, old, old man sitting up against a tree. The old man's white hair sparkled in the sunlight as he sat with his arms crossed and his head resting on his arms.

The surprised traveler ran right up to the old man and asked, "Excuse me, excuse me, are you OK?"

The old man didn't move and gave no response. The traveler got down on one knee and touched the man's shoulder, asking again, "Excuse me, are you OK?" Again, he got no response!

The traveler stood up to leave and, without warning, the old man's head raised, his eyes wide open. In a weak, creaky old voice he said: "Just keep traveling; you are on the right road. Before you cross the river, gather up all that you can of what you find there, because you can never go back." His eyes closed and his head dropped once again to rest on his arms.

The traveler waited, then finally turned and continued down the road in the hot sun, telling himself the old man must be crazy. Then he thought about what the old man had said and laughed to himself. "There probably isn't even a river!"

The traveler continued walking and finally came to a huge hill. When he reached the top, he saw a big, beautiful river flowing swiftly at the bottom of the road. Excited, he raced down the hill and jumped right into the cool water. Scooping the water into his hands, he threw it into the air and danced around as the drops fell on him. Suddenly he stopped, as the old man's words came back to him: "Before you cross the river, gather up all that you can of what you find there because you can never go back."

Looking around, the traveler saw nothing except the usual twigs, stones, and reeds of grass. He thought, "The only things to gather here would be these stones, but why would I need these? Maybe to fight off a wild animal, but I really don't think so." But he bent down anyway and gathered some stones and placed them in his pocket. Then he turned to cross the river, but before he did, he stopped and thought, "This is the craziest *thing I have ever done." Then he crossed the river.*

The sky grew dark, and the traveler became tired. So he decided to get off the trail and set up a small camp. He quickly fell fast asleep. About midnight, he awoke sharply and stood up. He gazed at the full moon that lit up the whole sky. But he grew angry when he realized what had awakened him. He had rolled over on that ridiculous handful of stones in his pocket. So he reached in to pull out the stones and toss them away. As he did so, the light of the moon caught the stones. To his amazement, they had all turned into precious gems – diamonds, emeralds, rubies, and sapphires! Then he had a moment of regret as he thought, "I wish I had gathered more before I crossed the river."

Explain to your students: *"This class is like the river bank, littered with stones that may turn into precious gems if you pick them up. Just as the old man couldn't make the traveler gather as many stones as his pockets would hold, neither can I make you gather the nuggets of wisdom offered here. Nor can anyone else. I can and will, however, encourage you to gather up as much knowledge as you can before you cross the river because you can never come back to this moment."* (And with that, pull from your pocket a handful of sparkling colored glass 'gems' – one for each student.)

What a great way to begin a new class. John LeTellier, master Quantum Teacher, facilitator and storyteller, creates a sensory-rich experience in the design and telling of his Gem Story. He includes three key elements which can be woven throughout any teaching: metaphor, imagery and suggestion.

Metaphor

Our brains are meaning-making machines, searching for matches to previous experiences. "Most of our normal conceptual system is metaphorically structured; that is, most concepts are partially understood in terms of other concepts" (Lakoff and Johnson, 1980, p. 56). Metaphors can liven up otherwise forgettable concepts, tapping them into the brain easily and quickly with association. Examples:

FINISHING TOUCHES

- Metaphor
- Imagery
- Suggestion

- school as a journey (gem story),

- tests and quizzes as performances. As with a professional athlete, all the talent in the world is only as valuable as that person's performance on the court or field.

Imagery

Visual imagery and memory are profoundly powerful, as we discussed earlier. For example, DON'T picture a white hippopotamus with green stripes. You saw it anyway, didn't you? Your brain does this automatically. Neuro-scientists say that 90 percent of the brain's sensory input comes from visual sources and the brain has an immediate and natural response to symbols, icons and strong, simple images (Jensen, 1994). We can use this ability of the brain to our advantage.

> *90% of the brain's sensory input comes from visual sources*

Many subjects, such as math, offer an extra challenge to students who are concrete processors due to their highly abstract nature. When you create a distinctive image to explain a concept, it instantly goes from abstract to concrete – and is thus easier to understand. Examples:

- fractions shown as pieces of pizza

- Mind Maps

- graphic organizers

- acting out prepositions: in (climb in a box to say it), on (get on the table), around (hug the box).

Suggestion

The "power of suggestion" is profound; we use this phrase frequently and experience it daily – in advertising, verbal nuances and body language. Although we don't consciously dwell on it, our brains act as parallel processors; they can actually take in more information faster than we ever thought possible. As you learned in Chapter 4, everything in the classroom sends a message that either propels toward or detracts from learning. Everything speaks. Dr. Georgi Lozanov, father of suggestology, promotes the premise that every detail matters. From the tone of the

Chapter 4
page 66

voice to the arrangement of the chairs to the neatness of the environment – it all matters and affects the learning (Lozanov, 1978).

Our brains co-process information at incredible speeds, both consciously and "paraconsciously". Lozanov defines paraconscious as "everything that, for the given moment, is outside the scope of consciousness. . . and comprises peripheral perceptions (Lozanov, 1978, p.13)." These perceptions, or suggestions, are influenced by:

Chapter 2
page 19

Chapter 4
page 67

- our intentions (see Chapter 2)
- the use of peripherals, color and music in the environment (see Chapter 4)
- and the use of positive language, and nonverbals (see Chapter 6).

 Chapter 6
pages 117, 124

Imagine . . . and suddenly the experience Colin just had, not only makes perfect sense, but has a whole new meaning, based on what just happened. Inside Colin's head, a light bulb blinks on. He's hooked because he's just experienced what FUN learning can be when it's set up that way!

REVIEW

REVIEW

Bridge the gap between you and your students – by *design*. In every learning design, you can easily enroll them, set them up for success, and tap into their every intelligence and modality!

Take a moment to envision yourself entering their world, then leading them effortlessly into your world of content, then back to theirs, transformed. Hear students anticipating, participating and demonstrating their unleashed genius. Feel the excitement as students go for it in their learning like never before – with relevance, clarity and engagement cemented into their experience.

What elements in your design will set them up for this kind of success? See yourself as you gently take them from large group to small group to individual with visual, auditory and kinesthetic learning. Hear yourself enrolling them, creating their experience of the learning, to create teachable moments. Students grab the information when they're at the edge of their seats, and they love it. They get to use their many intelligences as you suggest, model and paint success into their world.

CELEBRATE

I Know!

Check the box if you know how to use:

- ❏ Modalities V-A-K
- ❏ The Success Model
- ❏ EEL Dr. C, The Quantum Teaching Design Frame
- ❏ The Multiple Intelligences
- ❏ Use of Metaphor, Imagery and Suggestion

Celebrate! *Powerful Learning and Success You Design!*

Orchestrating Success Through Content

THE PERFORMANCE BEGINS

Now that you have all the necessary tools to create the optimal context for learning in your class, you're ready for the content. You've set the stage for the symphony and the performance is about to begin.

Content and context are equally important. As you've discovered in this book already, there's a lot more to context than meets the eye. The same is true for content. The curriculum you follow, like the musical score in a symphony, is a structural component of content, but it's just the beginning.

In Quantum Teaching, as in a symphony, the content includes the **presentation** – succinct yet passionate, elegant yet engaging. Any item of a curriculum, like any bit of music, can be dry and lifeless or dynamic and vibrant. Master presenters, be they kindergarten teachers or motivational speakers, have definite strategies and techniques to ensure that their presentations have impact. In Part II, you'll learn those very strategies and techniques.

Another element of the content in a symphony is the conductor's masterful **facilitation** of the orchestra, tapping the musical talent in each musician and the music-making potential in each instrument. Like musicians and their music, the students and curriculum can be arranged in harmony and synchronicity, following the learning's dynamic design. In the symphony hall, the way musicians and music are facilitated can lead to a level of performance beyond the composer's expectation. In the classroom, the way you facilitate students and curriculum can lead to performance that's just as delight-fully surprising as an inspired rendition by an orchestra of musical prodigies. Part II gives you the strategies to create such results.

Just as a skillful conductor builds the skills and enriches the lives of the musicians by expanding their reper-toire, you can enrich your students' lives by expanding the repertoire of their **learning and life skills.** At SuperCamp, we've developed strategies and skill-building techniques that not only enable students to far exceed their previous performance levels, but also to greatly improve their per-sonal interactions with others. Blended easily into the cur-riculum you teach, these learning and life skills give your students the edge that propels them ahead as Quantum Learners and Communicators.

Orchestrating Powerful Presentation

ENROLL

What if

you could teach more, faster, and increase the impact of what you say?

What if students hung on your every word? What if you spoke with such clarity that there was little room for misunderstanding? What would happen if your joy and passion about learning radiated through all you said and did? What would be the impact on your students? What would be the impact on you?

Imagine . . . Colin leans slightly forward, thinking intently about the information on the board. His hands shape the concept as he calls back the key phrase in unison with his classmates. His teacher moves about the classroom with confidence and speaks with an inviting tone. Randomly, she weaves students' names into the examples. Her volume, intonation and pacing act as currents on which she "floats" the content.

EXPERIENCE

Finally, the concept settles in as Colin relates it to an experience he had while learning to roller-blade.

Suddenly he sees the information with greater clarity. His teacher, it seems, knows how to focus Colin's attention and connect him with associations that can help him understand. Colin hears himself say, "I get it!" A smile peeks from the edges of his lips. Although this class is Colin's most challenging, he senses his teacher's commitment to his success, her patience with his learning pace and her tenacity to hold him to his best ability.

SEVEN GUIDELINES TO PRESENTATION SUCCESS

1 KNOW WHAT YOU WANT
Know specifically what you want to occur during each part of the learning process. Know the cognitive, affective and physical objectives for each activity. Clarity leads to success.

2 BUILD RAPPORT
Be committed to your students. Get to know them. Know their backgrounds, interests, past failures and successes. This builds your credibility and provides bridges into their world.

3 "READ" THEM
Watch for clues in behavior, attitude and language that would provide information on your students' current states. Ask them for in-the-moment feedback regarding the teaching's effect, the thoughts it provoked, and reactions it stimulated so you can execute adaptations to your lessons based on students' needs.

4 TARGET THEIR STATE
All learning is state-dependent. Orchestrate students' states to set them up for success. Know the target state for each learning activity. Change their states until they reach the target state.

5 REACH THEIR MODALITY
Through language patterns, voice, gestures and activities, tap into the visual, auditory and kinesthetic modalities of your students.

6 USE THE SPACE
All the room's a stage! Use a variety of spots as anchors: presenting, storytelling, feedback, initial instruction, conferencing.

7 BE REAL
Present an authentic, congruent message of openness, honesty and fairness.

THE MOST POWERFUL ACT A TEACHER CAN PERFORM

We'll focus now on the deliverer of the curriculum: you. You represent one of the most significant and influential factors in your students' success as learners. Dr. Georgi Lozanov states that the most powerful act you can perform for your students is to **model** what it means to be a learner (Lozanov, 1979). Your modeling, authenticity, congruence and availability empower and inspire students to unleash the potential they possess as learners.

Remember:
Everything speaks; what you say and how you say it.

So in this chapter you'll learn how to maximize your ability to model. You'll take a look at what we call "congruent communication," and be reminded that what you say and how you say it make a huge difference in how your students receive your curriculum. You'll discover distinctions about the words you speak and the impact they have on your students. You'll explore the effect of suggestion as a powerful tool to increase student buy-in. Finally, you'll learn how to utilize your voice, face, body and words to increase your speaking effectiveness.

ARE YOU A QUANTUM TEACHER?

Your ability to communicate, in combination with an effective learning design, provides a dynamic learning experience for your students. But first let's discuss what a Quantum Teacher is and does. What characterizes teachers who get quantum results with their students? Take a moment to review the list below. Use it as a personal inventory. On a 3-point scale (1=low, 2=average, 3=high) rate yourself on each of these characteristics:

- Enthusiastic: exhibits a zest for life
- Commanding: mobilizes people
- Positive: sees the opportunity in every moment
- Personable: builds rapport easily with a variety of students
- Humorous: appropriately lighthearted about mistakes
- Flexible: finds more than one way to reach outcomes
- Accepting: looks beyond outward actions and appearances to find core values
- Articulate: communicates clearly, succinctly and truthfully
- Sincere: has positive intentions and motives
- Spontaneous: can go with the flow and still maintain the outcomes
- Interesting and Interested: connects information to students' life experiences and cares about who the students are
- Holds students "able": believes in and orchestrates for their success
- Sets and maintains high expectations: establishes guidelines for quality of relationships and quality of work that require everyone's best effort.

A Quantum Teacher orchestrates learning according to the modalities and styles of his or her learners. A Quantum Teacher teaches life skills in the midst of academic skills, molding the mental / physical / spiritual attributes of the students. A Quantum Teacher places high priority on the interactions in the learning environment, paying attention to the quality of interactions among learners, between the learners and their teacher, and of the learners with the curriculum.

Remember our definition of *quantum*: "Interactions that transform energy into radiance." The Quantum Teacher uncovers the natural energy within each student and orchestrates interactions that transform that energy into radiance for others.

Ideal? Unrealistic? Not really. Many teachers just like you exhibit these traits every day. The question is, how consistently do they display these traits? Getting extraordinary results from ordinary people takes consistency and congruency. That means consistently employing the highest level of delivery, and establishing congruency between what we believe about students' incredible capacity to learn and the ways in which we present the curriculum. (see Chapter Three for beliefs of a Quantum Teacher). This consistency and congruency must happen day-in, day-out, moment-to-moment to transform the daily school experience into a life-enhancing event. Let's look into specific strategies and techniques you can use to maintain high levels of consistency and congruency.

Chapter 3
pages 52, 60

b MODALITY MATCHING

The brain contains three major freeways, or modalities, for processing the stimuli that come at us from the world outside ourselves. These three modalities – visual, auditory and kinesthetic – are actually communication conduits that help you make sense of your world. The connection between the words you say and the ways you internally represent your world make it essential that you pay careful attention to your speech patterns. Using predicates and phrases that match each modality strengthens your students' receptivity. You can literally speak to the modality of learning that best supports the kind of thinking you want to elicit. For example, see how the following sentences create images in your mind:

Picture this: A smiling, pink elephant in green high tops poses near the park bench. This word "picture" signals the brain to utilize the visual modality. The picture is strengthened by color words and the prepositional phrase.

Listen to how this phrase *rings true*: You understand the instructions only after you have assembled the wagon. The words "listen" and "rings true" cues the auditory modality.

Get the feel for this next point as you *grasp* its application: "Get", "feel" and "grasp" capture the kinesthetic modality.

Here are a few modality-specific phrases you can use to elicit modality-specific associations:

Visual: I see what you mean. It's clear now. Picture this. Look! Imagine.

Auditory: Rings true. Sounds good to me. Listen! Say it again.

Kinesthetic: Get a hold of this. Feels right. Tackle this!

FOUR PRINCIPLES OF POWERFUL COMMUNICATION

Remember, everything you say elicits specific associations. Notice the associations created as you read the following:

"OK, class, stop talking and quit being so distracted. As you know, this class is getting harder and harder as the days go by. The content is extremely confusing, and most students have a difficult time even getting a C, so if you're expecting anything higher than a C, you'd better buckle down and work harder and longer.

"What I want you to do now is take out your homework from last night, and then you should pass them this way." (After looking over the papers. . . .) *"I can see already that I don't like the way you did this. I'm obviously going to have to teach this to you again.*

"Today, I'm going to give you a choice: we can either keep trudging through this material by my lectures or you can try to understand it on your

FOUR PRINCIPLES FOR POWERFUL COMMUNICATION:
- Elicit the Image
- Direct the Focus
- Be Inclusive
- Be Specific

own by reading it. Now it's important to note that most students fail this next section because it is so advanced."

Compare that to this:

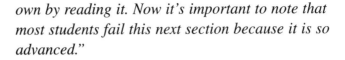

"Good day, class. Please be seated and focus this way. We are entering a portion of our curriculum that is easily the most challenging part. I know you have the ability to do well. Please know that students like yourselves have done very well on this part, especially when they remember to ask questions and participate.

"Let's begin where we left off with last night's HomeFun. Please locate it, and then pass it to your right." (After collecting and reviewing the papers...) *"It looks as though we would benefit from a quick review of yesterday's concept. Is that an accurate assumption?"* (pause) *"Great. Go ahead and take out your notes, and let's review using the example from yesterday.*

"Oh, by the way, after our little refresher this morning, I thought we might approach our next portion of curriculum a bit differently. Can we talk about it after the review?" (pause) *"Thanks."*

We hope you noticed a big difference between these examples. Powerful communication can be intentional and easy. With every interaction you have in the classroom, how you say things is just as important as what you say, maybe even more so. When you teach, give directions, set context or give feedback, remember these four principles:

- Elicit the Image

- Direct the Focus

- Be Inclusive

- Be Specific

Elict the Image

Try this little experiment: Do not think of a gorilla. Don't notice the gorilla is wearing purple Spandex tights, green tennis shoes and a baseball cap. OK, end of experiment.

What happened? In order to not think of the colorfully-clad gorilla, you had to create the image first. Your brain naturally creates, edits, stores and retrieves images. This happens automatically, and is directly influenced by the words you hear. The human brain creates images constantly. This happens either through sensory input that's visual, auditory or both. When you hear words your brain immediately processes them as "images." These images or impressions begin a domino effect, setting off myriad associations. For example, when you hear "ball" your brain retrieves a variety of stored images: basketball, baseball, beach ball, volleyball, tennis ball, a formal dance, all in addition to seeing the letters b-a-l-l. Often, the associations created are contrary, or at least mis-aligned with the concepts in the communication being heard. It's only in context that we can choose the precise meaning of the concept. Therefore, it's imperative that you consciously choose words to convey an idea accurately. The words you choose greatly impact your desired outcome.

Use the brain's ability to provide rich associations to your advantage. Craft your words to elicit an image that can propel your students' learning.

> *"Class, this is the most difficult and tedious part of the chapter, so be cautious or you'll fail."*

What images does it create? Difficulty, tediousness, danger, failure. Notice how the images differ when you say,

> *"This is easily the most challenging portion of the chapter. Being attentive will ensure a clear understanding."*

You create in your students' minds the impression or image you have in your mind. Consciously choose words that ignite positive associations, propel learning and enhance your communication.

Two levels of processing: conscious, non-conscious

Direct the Focus

Similar to the first principle, Direct the Focus capitalizes on the brain's ability to sort through the deluge of sensory input and focus its attention. Scientists estimate that our brain receives over 10,000 bits of information every second we're awake. Wow! How do we handle all that input? One answer lies in the brain's dual processing capability. Once in the brain, the sensory information is processed, either on a conscious or non-conscious level (Lozanov, 1979).

Try this experiment: Notice the layout of this page. Notice the graphics, the format of the text, and how your eye is drawn to important information. Now notice the temperature of the room you're in. What happened? As you read the words, your mind focused on each point: the layout, the graphics, the design, and so on. Your mind then selected a particular input on which to focus, leaving the others, like the ambient temperature, non-conscious. But as soon as your attention was drawn to it, you zeroed in on the temperature and all the details of this page became non-conscious again in a split second.

How can this principle help you teach more effectively? Use Direct the Focus when giving directions. Ask yourself, "Where do I want my students to focus their attention?" Then choose the words that direct their focus.

"Stay away from the art supplies as you move to your group,"

brings attention to the art supplies. This increases the probability of someone noticing them. Instead, direct the focus, thus:

"Look to the place where your group meets. Please move directly to that spot, and take your books with you."

With no mention of the art supplies and a clear focus on where to go and what to bring, you decrease the chance of students discovering the art supplies.

Here's another example of Direct the Focus: Let's say you want to get your class' attention. Rather than saying,

"Stop talking," or *"I'm waiting,"* direct their focus.

"Please allow your eyes to look this direction and your body to face me."

Another example: Let's say you're teaching today's lesson and want students to recall information from yesterday. Provide a cognitive prompt by directing the focus to yesterday's highlights.

"Remember from yesterday the two elements in salt, and think of their symbols. Be ready when I call on you to tell us those two symbols."

Your words, intentionally or unintentionally, unlock associations. Since these associations occur in students' minds, we can direct them to the associations most likely to support learning.

Be Inclusive

Ever notice statements like these spoken in a classroom? "What I want you to do next is take out your books." "What you're going to do next is take out the homework from last night." "I need you to gather your materials." Teachers make statements like these hundreds of times a day. They clearly communicate the expected behavior, but what else do they communicate? If language elicits associations, what associations are being invited? Notice that the words "I want you to," "You're going to," and "I need you to" perpetuate a me-verses-you dynamic. The message behind them is, "I'm in control and you'll do what I say." Now, how might someone who has negative associations wrapped around teachers respond to that? Perhaps in a rebellious or less-than-cooperative manner? This negative association, even at the non-conscious level, has a dramatic effect on learning and behavior.

Now notice how the following statements create a more positive, propelling dynamic.

COMMON STATEMENTS REPHRASED

■ Don't forget your homework.
Remember to do your homework.

■ I need you to take out your books.
Let's take out our books.

■ I'm going to be teaching you the steps.
We'll be learning the steps.

■ Now we are at the difficult part of this unit.
This is easily the most challenging part you've mastered so far.

■ Don't talk.
Focus your attention to this spot.

■ For some of you this next section will be a breeze.
This section is a challenge in various degrees.

■ Look up here.
Catch this everyone.

"Let's take out our books." "Go ahead and take out your homework from last night." "It's time to gather our materials." A simple change in words fosters an inclusive, everyone-is-invited, collaborative relationship.

As a Quantum Teacher, you desire to create an atmosphere of collaboration, teamwork and inclusion especially knowing the negative associations some students have about the student/teacher dynamic. Being conscious and deliberate about the words you choose can strengthen the sense of togetherness and elicit positive associations. To support your intention to create a collaborative learning environment, use language that invites inclusion. "Let's," "us" and "we" create a sense of cohesion and unity. In effect, the words say, *"We're in this together."* Remember: everything speaks, always!

Be Specific

Let's say you want your class to get ready to leave for break. So you say, *"Everyone, please get ready for the break."* Students shove things in their desks or backpacks, toss materials onto the nearest counter and tuck trash under their seats or in the corner. Did they follow your instructions? Well, they did "get ready for break," yet it may not have been the way you intended. They misinterpreted your directions because you weren't specific.

Here's a helpful rule of tongue: Economy of Language. In other words, say what needs to be said with the greatest amount of clarity and the least amount of words.

Often miscommunication results from a generality. A generality allows room for the other person to fill in the blanks with his or her own interpretation. The more specific the request, the greater the chance it will be accomplished according to your intention. A more specific request for getting ready for break would achieve the result you had in mind.

hot tip

Say what needs to be said with the greatest amount of clarity and the least amount of words. It's economy of language.

Suppose you said,

"Everyone, please neatly return the materials to where you got them, put the trash in the basket, and replace your papers in the section labeled, 'project.'"

With the specifics spelled out, you increase the match between what you intended and what the words produce. Specificity provides clarity. Clarity promotes action.

Sometimes you may find it necessary to say more to clearly communicate, as in the previous example. Other times you may need to say less.

"What I want you to do next is take out your books and find the graph on page 134," can simply be stated, *"We'll focus on the graph on page 134. Please take out your books."*

Teachers often talk too much. They over-explain concepts, repeat directions and lengthen their answers in a way that dilutes the impact of what they say. Why do they do this? Often, because of a lack of clarity; they're unsure about what they want to say.

Here's one way to avoid this trap: Begin direction-giving statements with an *action* verb: take, draw, write, move, talk, etc. Not only do you get right to the point, you also set student behavior in motion. In addition, you may find it helpful to use a cueing phrase in your direction statement.

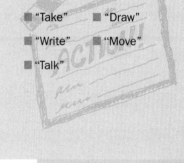

"When I say 'go,' move to your team location and be seated. Go!"

The cueing phrase let's students know when the directions begin and you'll avoid having to speak over the sounds of moving bodies. Also, take a moment to organize your thoughts before you speak. What seems like forever as you stand before your class is actually only a few moments from the students' perspective. Take your time. Say what needs to be said. Better to say it well the first time than to restate it after the associations have already been made in your students' minds. When you couple the Four Principles with your use of modality predicates, you'll be amazed at your students' responsiveness.

GET TO THE POINT:
Begin direction-giving statements with an action verb:

■ "Take"   ■ "Draw"

■ "Write"   ■ "Move"

■ "Talk"

NON-VERBAL COMMUNICATIONS

DEMONSTRATE

Do this: Slouch in your chair, slow down your breathing, lower your head and let your eyes look down. Say, "I'm so excited."

Now sit up, lean slightly forward, brighten your eyes, breathe from your chest, smile and say, "I'm so excited!"

What difference did you notice? Did the second "I'm so excited!" contain more energy and life? Why? Because congruence existed between the message and the body language. Your body and voice are carriers that propel your message. With the effective use of facial expressions, gestures, voice and posture, you can send a congruent message that strengthens your communication. A congruent message is one in which your words, facial expression, gestures and posture all align. Your face says the same thing your body is saying and your mind is thinking.

Use these questions to help you craft a congruent message:

Keeping in mind the Four Principles of Powerful Communication (Elicit the Image, Direct the Focus, Be Inclusive and Be Specific), rewrite the following sentences:

- I want you to find your study group and sit together.
- You need to get better grades.
- No talking.
- Let me explain this.
- You should never slam your book shut.
- Try not to be late to my class.

- What outcome do I desire?

- What state do I want my learners in?

- What state do I need to access that supports the desired outcome?

- How can I use my eyes, face, voice, hands and posture to communicate this state?

Eye Contact

Think of a time when you listened to someone speak who hardly ever looked at you. Now think of a time when a speaker looked at you while she spoke. During which time did you feel more included?

Frequent eye contact establishes and maintains high levels of rapport. Look at your students, but hold your glance no longer than three seconds with a particular person. Any longer than about three seconds often gets interpreted as "the stare." Avoid looking across the tops of students' heads. Make a conscious effort to communicate with each student during the lesson using your eyes.

Facial Expressions

Your face is a powerful communicator. The non-verbal messages sent through raised eyebrows, a smile, a wrinkled forehead, nods, wide eyes and an open mouth are worth many words. What may feel exaggerated to you speaks clearly to the class. Use your face in an obvious way to communicate the feeling of your message.

A little practice might be useful. For each of the following words, make an exaggerated facial expression: wonder, surprise, warmth, care, inquisitiveness, fear, happiness. How did you do? Were you able to make the expressions distinct from one another? Continue practicing with surprise, joy, openness and intrigue.

A word of caution and a reminder, however: Because of the nature of classroom dynamics, teachers often think on their feet, creating instructions, analogies and explanations on the spot. We affectionately call this "winging it." As you form your thoughts, your face naturally relaxes into a facial phenomenon called " flat affect," a no-emotion expression. Because this automatically occurs each time you internally construct your thoughts, remember to make a conscious effort to smile, especially when you're thinking on your feet. You might have one of those faces that naturally relaxes into a deceiving frown. Perhaps when you have no expression on your face you look mad, sad or disappointed. It's rare to see your face in a no-expression state. It often occurs when you're brushing your teeth, fixing your hair and posing. Check it out the next time you're busy in the mirror. See what's there. Then feel free to practice that award-winning smile of yours.

Voice

Your face-voice congruency provide a tool equally as powerful as your facial expressions. Ever been put off by the *way* someone said something, despite their positive words? Tone, volume and rate are the spices of communication, adding flavor to your face and gestures. Tone, the inflection and pitch quality of your voice, can express joy, disappointment, doubt, certainty and tentativeness, as well as other

DEMONSTRATE

emotions. Volume quickly captures the auditory sense. Softness often communicates importance, as in a secret or a key point. Loudness speaks of excitement, command and attention.

Variations in rate, or speed, enhance the importance of your message, punctuating significant phrases. Varying your rate with frequent pauses, steady cadences and quick clauses keeps students engaged while adding interest and anticipation to your message.

Vocal variety influences even the most mundane information. Use whispers for your most important points. Use quick, short sentences to build excitement. A medium-paced, rhythmic speech pattern appeals to the auditory learners. Also, the movement of your head and face will assist in voice variation. For practice, videotape yourself saying the sentence, "I am a capable, competent and inspiring teacher." Say it with different intonations, volume, pacing, facial expressions and head movements. Play it back and close your eyes. Listen carefully to how each sentence sounds. Choose the one you like best. Play that one again with your eyes open.

Gestures

Natural and purposeful hand, arm and body motions accentuate your message, punctuate key statements and capture the attention of kinesthetic learners by providing animation to your voice. Be sure to move your arms and hands outside the vertical lines established by your body frame. Imagine two lines drawn vertically from your shoulders to the floor. Often gestures are contained within these lines. Gestures outside these lines send a message of invitation and inclusion. Use an open palm when gesturing toward individuals. This invites participation and partnership while suggesting "take my hand." Pre-determined and purposeful hand motions can visually represent an idea. Here are a few examples:

- Show the number of the point you're making: *"This is the second idea proposed by Whitman,"* as you hold up two fingers.

- Draw a picture frame in the air to represent the concept of framing your ideas for writing.

- Turn one hand over while saying, *"On the one hand,"* and turn the other hand over while saying, *"On the other hand."*

Think of how you would use hand motions to support the following statements:

- The second reason for the fall of the Roman Empire . . .
- To close up this problem, let's . . .
- In the center of a cell is the nucleus.

Posture

Have you ever sat on a bench in a park or a mall and watched people go by? Take yourself there for a moment. Imagine this: a small child goes racing by, giggling hysterically. She quickly glances behind her, nearly stumbles, then keeps running with renewed vigor. Meanwhile, at the phone booth a man stands slouched over, clutching the phone. His head nearly rests on his chest as he scuffs his shoe against the post. He nods methodically and slowly hangs up the phone. In these scenes how would you describe the mood or feelings of each person? On what did you base your conclusion? Their postures, of course. The body communicates the internal condition of the mind. Think of it this way: posture is the framing or scaffolding on which your facial expressions, voice and gestures find their support.

Particular postures denote specific messages. Comfortableness with your own body, its movement and stature, causes your students to be more at ease. Dancing and theatrics are two arenas some Quantum Teachers use to practice body fluency and execution. Whether or not you have the body of the fitness instructor at the nearby gym is irrelevant. What matters is how you carry yourself – the way you hold your body and move it through space. You wear your attitude like clothing on your body. How you feel and what you think shows up in your posture. If the current unit of study, the assembly, or the film don't interest you, your students will

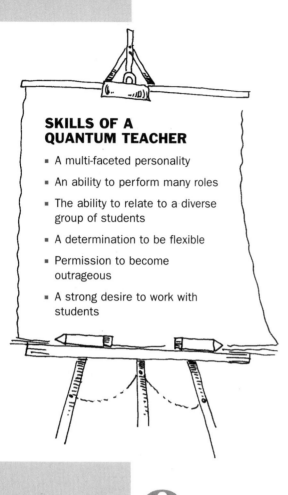

SKILLS OF A QUANTUM TEACHER

- A multi-faceted personality
- An ability to perform many roles
- The ability to relate to a diverse group of students
- A determination to be flexible
- Permission to become outrageous
- A strong desire to work with students

know. Conversely, what excites you and brings out your passion translates to your posture.

How often do you take a natural stance of wonder, openness and discovery while teaching? Dial up your awareness about what your posture says. Videotaping provides an excellent mirror. Tape yourself for an entire class period. Then spend some time assessing the congruency of your message with your nonverbal communication. Watch films of confident presenters like Martin Luther King or John F. Kennedy with the sound off. Notice how they move their body and position it to make certain key points. Stand and emulate them. It may feel a bit awkward at first, but with this practice you're simply building skills to strengthen your communication effectiveness.

e EFFECTIVE PRESENTATION PACKAGES

Imagine this: You're in your classroom and have just completed the lesson. You give directions that include students moving to their learning teams. Very few people move, so you repeat the directions. Everyone now moves. As you navigate through the room you notice that many students' notes are incomplete and in fact are missing the most important point.

How did this happen? You know you emphasized that important point and gave clear directions. What did you miss? It might be as simple as the package you used to deliver the information and the directions. Think of a package as a composition of separate elements working together, similar to a gift. You've got the container, the wrapping, the ribbon and the bow. All of these elements work together to form the package.

This is also true of presenting. Direction-giving has a distinct look, sound and feel. Likewise, inspiring your students to greatness sounds and looks different than presenting information. To maximize your impact, it's important to make distinctions between the kinds of communication you deliver.

There are moments when you teach, give directions, and provide inspiration. All are distinct from one another. These distinctions are organized into three presentation packages: Discoverer, Leader and Director. Each presentation package consists of specific language patterns, posture and gestures.

Let's get a better feel for each of these presentation packages. They'll enhance your ability to communicate and increase your results with students.

Discoverer

Imagine yourself in one of your best teaching moments. Replay the video. That's right; allow yourself to be fully there for a moment. Remember the place, the looks on your learners' faces. Listen to yourself talking, and sense your gestures. You feel alive, engaged and enthusiastic about the material you're presenting. Now, press *pause* on this imaginary video. Take a look at your expression, your gestures and your posture. What do you notice? Most likely, you're light on your feet, leaning slightly forward as your excitement lifts you.

As the video continues, notice how you move toward, then away from the participants, beckoning them, enticing them into new discoveries. Your gestures, voice and expressions congruently convey intrigue and wonder. You hear yourself saying, *"Hey, check this out. Listen carefully to what happens next. Take a look at this. See it this way. Notice how this fits together with this. Is all this becoming clearer now, or what!"* You exude an air of purposeful playfulness, full of childlike curiosity.

As the video continues, you consciously mix visual, auditory and kinesthetic predicates and postures, sometimes standing straight and tall, other times bending slightly at the knees and making gestures that say, "Come this way." Your voice changes pace and volume, amplifying your points with whispers and inflections. A quick pan of your learners reveals attentive postures, curious looks and nodding heads. You are in the zone, the Discovery Zone. You're presenting in the Discoverer Package. Feels natural, doesn't it? When you're

DISCOVERER

To elicit curiosity, wonder, excitement and a sense of discovery, deliver your content using the following characteristics:

- Stand lightly on your feet
- Lean slightly forward
- Move laterally across the front of the room
- Maintain an air of discovery and fascination
- Use visual, auditory and kinesthetic predicates
- Use "let's," "us" and "we" to build inclusion.

interested in what you're teaching, excited about the content and anxious for all your students to be as interested in the information as you are, your gestures, voice, and expressions send a congruent messag: "Discover this!"

Employ this presentation package when you present information, especially new learning. Notice your entire countenance and demeanor radiates with curiosity, wonder, intrigue, excitement and discovery. As you exhibit these traits, watch them surface in your learners.

Leader

Again, think back to the times you've heard dynamic leaders speak. You might remember Dr. Martin Luther King's "I Have a Dream" speech, or President Kennedy's "Ask not what your country can do for you . . . " State of the Union address. These men, like many other motivating, inspiring leaders, spoke from personal passion. The inward fountain of values and beliefs flows outward through specific gestures, postures and language patterns.

There are times, often spontaneous and serendipitous, when the situation calls for you to unify and inspire your group of learners toward commitment and action. This could be as simple and mundane as motivating students to pick up the trash – or a more futuristic enticement about graduating from school.

LEADER
To inspire and motivate students to a higher level of performance:

■ Stand straight, feet shoulder-length apart

■ Keep one foot in front of the other

■ Turn slightly toward one side of the audience at a time

■ Breathe fully

■ Maintain eye contact

■ Use primarily visual and kinesthetic predicates

Imagine this scene for a moment. Until recently, your class has demonstrated tenacity and self-motivation. They've tackled the most challenging parts of your curriculum with perseverance. Lately, however, you've sensed a change. Your class has lost the drive for excellence and seems content with mediocrity, complacent with just getting by. Like a coach whose team is losing at half-time, you size up the situation. You know what they need. You know they have what it takes. You also know it's up to them. What's the best thing to say? How should your very next words be presented? The answer: with passion, conviction and leadership.

You stand before your class, make eye contact with each person, and take a deep breath.

"Class, we've got a challenge ahead of us.

Challenges are nothing new to you. You've met this year's challenges with determination and have conquered each in turn. You've got what it takes. This is the time of year when it's easy to kick back, let it ride, put it in neutral." (You shift your weight to one foot, step slightly forward, and turn to speak to half of the group.)

"We've accomplished much up until now and I'm as proud of you as you are of yourselves. You've shown commitment and perseverance." (Now your weight shifts to the other foot and you turn to address the other half the room.)

"You've gone farther than you've ever gone in your academic lives. You've proven to yourselves that you can learn quickly, and . . . we've come together as a team to support each person in being our best."

(You stand squarely now, leaning forward.) *"Let's continue to give everything we do our highest effort and continue to convince ourselves of our incredible potential."*

The Leadership Package calls forth in us our deepest convictions and highest hopes for the students we teach, and communicates with directness and inspiration. Our students need us at times to call them to their higher selves; to draw out the potential we see; to restore faith. Although the above example may seem a bit contrived, your knowledge of your students, combined with your sincere desire to see them succeed, are the necessary ingredients you'll need to lead them to commitment and action.

Director

Different from Discoverer and Leader, the Director Package adds punch and precision to your direction-giving. Often directions are not carried out to your satisfaction because the directions lacked all the information, or lacked a distinct enough variation from your normal teaching voice. Have you ever given a set of directions only to have to retell them many times? Or stated the directions, set your students

DIRECTOR

To set students in motion:

- Stand straight.
- Square shoulders.
- Maintain eye contact.
- Use strong voice and pleasant face.
- Lace sentences with visual, auditory and kinesthetic predicates.

- In about 60 seconds . . .
- Please pause.
- In a moment you'll have the opportunity to . . .
- Stand up. (Make your body and voice congruent with statement.)
- When the music starts.
- When I say go . . .
- Everyone look up, look down, look front and clap.
- You have two minutes to . . .
- Please wrap it up . . . and thank your partner.
- You'll be interested to know the following:
- There are three things to know for your success on this task.

off to task and watched them scatter to a variety of interpretations? You can avoid these scenarios by crafting your directions so they are complete, succinct and presented with certainty. In the Director mode, students are mobilized into action, aligned and clear about the task.

Use these five elements when designing and delivering your directions:

When: Start with when you want people to do something, for example, *"In about 45 seconds, when I say, 'Go!'"* In this way, you provide listeners with the information as to whether or not they need to act immediately. You also prevent students from standing up to do something else before you've finished giving complete directions.

Who: Be specific about the person or persons to whom the directions apply, so that these individuals pay extra attention. *"Everyone will . . .,"* *"This half of the room will . . ."*

Directions: Give specific, succinct, just-in-time information that students need to accomplish the task or portion of the task. If possible, write the key information on the board, flip-chart or overhead. Otherwise repeat the directions in different words with different tonality. *"Discuss the three themes of Chapter 15, and complete your learning logs for today. Move into your learning teams."*

Check: Check the level of understanding. Ask, *"What questions do you have about this?"* Or ask them what box of understanding they are in: 1) Have questions; 2) Understand it; or 3) Could teach it.

Action: Finish the directions with a congruent call to action. Let students know when to begin. Use, *"Go"* *"Begin"* *"Let's get busy"* *"Get on it"* *"Engage"* or any other appropriate starter. When presenting the directions do so with body language that commands attention yet maintains dignity and rapport. Begin your sentences with action verbs: *"Take out your books."* *"Grab a pencil."* *"Look in this direction."* *"Notice the chart on page 15."* *"Write this down."*

ANCHORING

Imagine this. Flames dance warmly atop the piled wood as the smoke trails past tall fir trees into the clear starlit sky. White marshmallows, soon to be nestled between graham crackers and chocolate, bob from bent coat hangers, and roast to a golden brown. Singing invades the night air amidst giggles and hugs.

What associations, feelings, thoughts came to mind as you read the previous paragraph? For many the sights and smells of a campfire evoke feelings of togetherness, warmth, relaxation. Many everyday occurrences elicit predictable responses: a police siren; lyrics from an old song; smells of a hospital room; desks in rows before a dusty chalkboard. These "anchors" serve to make life familiar, known, predictable. You can use the power of anchoring to elicit useful associations and positive responses from your students. Similar in impact as presentation packages and languaging on student engagement, anchoring promotes smooth transitions and optimal learning states.

Anchoring, from Neuro-Linguistics, can be defined as an associated response to a given stimulus. We experience many natural anchors: the crack of a baseball bat; flashing red lights; a song on the radio. These experiences elicit thoughts, memories and feelings. This happens all the time in your class. From the place you stand, to the motions you make, students are conditioned to elicit a certain state or give a certain response. You can use this to your advantage. We'll take a look at three anchors most useful for teaching and learning: personal, location and verbal.

Personal Anchor

Many athletes, performers, actors and speakers use the power of anchoring to maximize their performance. Here's how it's done: Let's say you wanted to anchor your best teaching moments, so that when you're feeling less than your best, you could pull yourself into a more resourceful state. First, take a deep breath. Think back to a moment when you were at

Record your personal anchor. Jot down the images and words that describe your "best moment".

your best – students were engaged, you were in strong rapport and the content was seamless. What were you thinking? Perhaps something such as: "I enjoy this!" "They're with me." "I know this material." "What's my next outcome?" What were you feeling? Perhaps you experienced joy, passion, excitement, curiosity. Be as present in that moment as you can. Notice where you are, what you're doing and the sounds you hear. Choose a word that represents this moment. A word like power, happiness or joy. Now clench your fist when you actually feel the moment come alive again, and say your word. Replay this "best moment" video, and again at the moment of an emotional connection clench your fist while saying your word. You have now established an anchor for your best teaching moment. Take the next few moments and replay the video over and over again. Each time remember to clench your fist and repeat the word.

Now imagine one of your less-than-best teaching episodes. As you do, clench your fist and feel the associations from your best moment envelop you.

This is a personal anchor, one that causes you to access the best of what you have to offer. Use this technique as you begin each class, when you're feeling inadequate for the task at hand, or even in the midst of a discouraging moment. You have the ability to access a powerful, resourceful state. Use your personal anchor to do that.

Location Anchors

Watching a skilled, dynamic speaker shows how location anchors work. Often, they shift from point to point actually taking a step to portray transition to the next point. In addition, another place on the platform (or even to the side of the podium) is used only for anecdotes or jokes. Soon, each time the speaker moves to that location, the audience is anticipating a story or joke.

Special Bulletin:
Your actions speak louder than your words!

Instruction Spot

This technique is useful in your classroom as well. Michael Grinder, Director of Educational Neuro-Linguistics, says that "when a teacher consistently uses certain nonverbals with a concept or idea, then the non-verbals and the concept are associated" (Grinder, 1991, p. 165). The front of the class is traditionally the instructional spot. It's where the overhead is projected, the whiteboard is placed, the demonstrations are performed. Students know that when you're in this place it's time to listen for knowledge, facts, inquires, etc. (This instructional spot is especially powerful when you use the Discoverer package with inclusive, enticing language.) You'll be amazed at the conditioned response of your students. As you move into the instructional spot, many students pick up a pen and prepare to take notes.

"Discipline" Spot

To the side of the room, or near your posted rules and agreements, is the "discipline" spot. It's here students receive feedback regarding their actions. You lower your voice, slow down your speaking rate, breathe and stand still. Purposeful eye contact with many of the students captures their attention as well. Using O.T.F.D. as your communication frame (see Chapter 9) you act as a " mirror" and provide students with the information they need to make corrections in attitude, behavior, speech, etc. After a few times at this anchor, students know what happens in that spot. Simply moving to that spot during a disruption in your teaching evokes a more focused, attentive state.

Chapter 9 page 201

Story Spot

A corner of your room could be reserved for stories or jokes. It's here that you enter story mode with inflected voice, grand gestures and exaggerated facial expressions for each character. As you begin to tell the story, notice how students shift their bodies to a sitting-up and leaning-forward position or even a leaned-back relaxed position.

Hot Tips Spot

You can even anchor a special place to deliver key ideas or hot tips. Known as the Hot Tips Spot, it is marked by a large X on the floor stage left at the front of the room. As you near the X encourage students to sit up, lean forward and listen intently. Step onto the spot, lower your voice to a whisper and deliver the key information, word, formula or other hot tip. It's an effective state change that increases attentiveness and concentration.

Modality Alleys

You can tap students' learning modalities by combining where you stand with what you say. Utilize the Discoverer Package for this anchor. Think of the front of your classroom as having three areas, or "alleys" marked out on the floor, running left to right: one at the front near the whiteboard; another just ahead of it; and one more just ahead of this. The first area, nearest the whiteboard is the **visual alley.** Here is where information is given, facts shared, formulas worked, etc. Here information is written or displayed. You stand tall, confident and use visually-loaded language: *"See what I mean?" "Here's the big picture." "This will be clear for you now."*

With a step or two forward you enter the **auditory alley.** Your voice inflections are more obvious and your speaking takes on a natural rhythm. Here explanations, anecdotes, analogies and metaphors are given to enhance the information given in the visual alley.

Another step or two forward is the **kinesthetic alley,** so named for the close proximity to the students. You can "reach out and touch" them. This alley is primarily reserved for direction-giving, instructing your students to form groups, move to different seats, stand and stretch, etc. It can also be used for heart felt stories or that occasional sit-on-the-student's-desk-we've-gotta-talk moment. Use the Director Package while in this alley. Your proximity and commanding directness mobilizes them into action. On the other hand, when telling an emotionally-gripping story (like a moment from the character's life, the conditions of trench life in WW I, or the loss of an electron during bonding) move closer to them. This tightens the feeling of

USE ANCHORING

- Personal
- Location
- Verbal

connection. Remember to slow down your rate of speaking and focus on kinesthetic words and phrases: *get, hold, grasp, feel, touch, envelop, wrap, enclose, snuggle,* as well as texture words: *smooth, rough, prickly, etc.*

As you gain facility with the distinctions in pace, posture, languaging, and purpose for each of the three alleys, you'll notice students matching you. As you enter the visual alley, they'll pick up a pen to jot down the information. As you begin an explanation, pens lift from the paper and students sit back a bit. Depending on your tone of voice and expressions, they'll either get ready to move or lean in for that great story as you step into the kinesthetic alley. By anchoring each of these spots you elicit a corresponding state. Try it! You'll like it!

Verbal Anchors

What you and the students say draws out certain associations. For example, when you say, "For your homework tonight…" what do students often do? Exactly, they groan. A useful state for learning? Not exactly. Instead make it a tradition, like Kevin T. Irvine, Colorado Teacher of the Year, does. He says, " homework" and the class erupts in applause and cheering! Sound radical? Perhaps, yet Kevin knows the power of anchoring associations.

Or this example. In response to the word "test," or "quiz," the class says, "C'mon, gimme that test!" with an air of confidence and strength of voice.

Think of key words or phrases you use that get a response from students. Create a verbal response that anchors positive associations and invites students to Act As If (more on this in Chapter 3, p. 52).

Rob Abernathy, master teacher, employed the use of a location anchor to ensure success for his substitute while he was away one day. Mr. A., as his students affectionately called him, established a place to the side of the class known as "The Spot." Each time the class would exceed the noise level or forget to keep an agreement like being on time, or having materials ready, he would walk calmly to "The Spot." Here Mr. A. would lower his voice, speak deliberately and call their attention to the inappropriate behavior. He prompted students to remind one another of the agreement and elicited ways to remedy the situation. Finally, the class would re-commit to the agreement, at which point they were directed to return to the task at hand.

As with most 4th/5th grade classes, a day with a substitute is a day to test the boundaries of behavior. Students arrived to class this particular day to find their desks rearranged. Not giving it much thought they took their seats, were greeted by the substitute, and the day began.

The next morning, Mr. A. arrived to find the substitute's report:

> *Mr. Abernathy:*
>
> *It was a pleasure to teach your class. They were respectful, cooperative and cordial. We accomplished the plans you left, and even had time for a review game and a special story I brought with me. I would enjoy substituting for you and your students in the future.*

Mr. A. smiled. It worked. He had arranged all the desks to face "The Spot."

Chapter 3 page 52

A LESSON FROM THE JAPANESE

Orchestrating the presentation of your curriculum is a high-level and useful skill. Since the curriculum often gets "handed down from heaven," it can be difficult to establish student buy-in. Hence, comments like: "Do we have to learn this?" "What does this have to do with anything?" "When will I ever use this?"

Your task as a Quantum Teacher: Present the curriculum with as much wonder, intrigue, fascination, and enthusiasm as you authentically can. Employing the skills of modality-matching, eliciting images, directing focus, inclusiveness and specificity with congruent nonverbals in distinguishable presentation packages adds clarity to your communication.

You've learned much in this chapter about orchestrating the presentation of your curriculum. Allow yourself to implement and gain ease with one element at a time. Start small. Begin with one part you know you can master quickly. And whatever you do, start. Great teachers believe in the power of "kaizen," the concept Japanese auto manufacturers live by: small, seemingly insignificant, continual and never-ending improvements. Congratulate yourself for being a great teacher who practices "kaizen."

You've grasped the fundamentals of dynamic presentations. From matching modalities to anchoring, from Elicit Images to Discoverer, from Directing Focus to body language. The fundamentals – modality matching, principles of communication, congruent body language, presentation packages and anchoring – in harmony with the Quantum Teaching Design Frame make you the maestro of student achievement.

> *Great teachers believe in the power of "kaizen," the concept many Japanese live by: small, seemingly insignificant, continual and never-ending improvements.*

I Know!

Check the box if you know how to use:

- ❏ Modalities Matching
- ❏ Eliciting Images
- ❏ Directing Focus
- ❏ Inclusiveness
- ❏ Specificity
- ❏ Voice
- ❏ Facial Expressions
- ❏ Gestures
- ❏ Posture
- ❏ Discoverer Package
- ❏ Leader Package
- ❏ Director Package
- ❏ Anchoring

Celebrate!

A Powerful presentation of your dynamic curriculum!

CELEBRATE

Orchestrating Elegant Facilitation

ENROLL

What if

students were more consistently engaged in their learning?

What if you could "make easy" their readiness and ability to learn?

EXPERIENCE

Imagine . . . *Colin glances at his watch and can't believe it – class is almost over! It feels like this class just started a minute ago! He marvels at this every day. This class races by, while classes with other teachers seem to move in slow motion. Colin also notices that he learns a lot more in this class than he does in others, even though the situations seem similar. He taps his watch, just to check, and wonders why . . .*

The answer to Colin's question might lie in one simple word: facilitation.

As we said in the previous chapter, as a Quantum Teacher you place high priority on the **interactions** within your learning environment. You pay attention to the quality of interactions between yourself and the learners, as well as what goes on among the learners themselves. Plus, you watch the interactions of the learners with the curriculum.

At this point you've got the design to create a dynamic Quantum Teaching lesson with the help of EEL Dr. C. We've also given you tips for presenting your curriculum elegantly. Now let's focus on facilitating the interactions between your learners and the curriculum.

Picture this scene: Students have been in class now for 20 minutes. The teacher has just concluded an interactive lecture, receiving minimal participation and multiple disruptions. He did his best to stimulate discussion, pose thought-provoking questions, even flash the main points on the overhead. Still, he got little participation. With 30 minutes remaining, he wonders what to do.

Has this scene ever played out in your classroom? When it happens, what do you do? How do you keep learners engaged with the curriculum? How do you maintain interest, keep focus and boost participation? How do you maximize the moments of learning that happen with your students?

Our answer is, you **orchestrate** the interaction between the learner and the curriculum. You facilitate – make easy – the level of participation you want.

First, always begin knowing what you want as a final result. Start with a clear vision of the outcome. This might be an outcome for the level of respect in class, the quality of work, the amount of time to complete a task, etc. Clearly knowing the outcome you want gives you the ability to stay on course, and facilitates your students' success.

So, how do you stay on course and keep the learner with you? Use the KEG! That's right **KEG.** When you read "keg", what came to mind? A large metal container filled with liquid refreshment? An old wooden barrel packed with gun powder? Right on both accounts. Utilize the three principles of KEG effectively and you'll avoid the explosion and enjoy the refreshment: **K**now what you want; **E**xplain what you want; **G**et what you want.

a REMEMBER THE KEG

Know It

The 'K' stands for **Know.** Know what you want. This might be a cognitive-based outcome such as "three factors leading to the fall of the Roman Empire," or a skill-based outcome such as "be prepared for class." Know what this outcome *looks* like (a chart listing the three factors with columns for events and consequences). Know what the outcome *sounds* like (students conversing with partners to complete the chart). Know what the outcome *feels* like (students calmly moving to the bookshelf to get information). The extent to which you know what the outcome looks, sounds and feels like is the extent to which you'll be able to communicate it clearly and get the results you want.

Explain It

The next principle of KEG is **Explain.** Once you clearly know the look, sound and feel of the outcome, explain it. Tell students how you envision it. Use the Four Principles of Powerful Communication – elicit positive images, direct their focus, be inclusive, and be specific. Example: Outcome – students move to learning groups. Package – Director. *"In just*

one moment, when I say 'groups,' stand up, take your note-books and texts, and move quickly and safely to the place your learning group meets. Remain standing and listen carefully for further instructions. Groups!"

A lack of results often stems from insufficient communication. Explain the expectations you have regarding quality of work, level of interpersonal interaction, use of resources, and so on. Here's another example: Outcome – In teams of three, students create a poster that visually represents the water cycle. Package – Director. *"The challenge is simple. The quality will be outstanding. Here's how it works. Visually represent the water cycle. You may use the poster paper and markers from the back table. Be sure your water cycle is in color, properly labeled, and includes as much detail as possible."*(These three quality characteristics are listed on the board/overhead.) *"Take 15 minutes to complete the poster. We'll do this in teams of three. Be sure you acknowledge each team member's ideas. Please look around and, with your eyes, locate the two people you'd want as fellow experts on this project. When I say 'water cycle,' gather in your groups and send one person to get your materials. Water cycle!"*

Get It

As students begin the task, you enter into the "G" of KEG: **Get it and Give feedback;** get the outcome. Watch and listen as students begin. Are they on the mark or not? Let them know. Give them feedback. Pause the class momentarily and let them know how they're doing. Better yet, elicit from students the necessary corrections, then resume.

Let's return to the above example. The students move into their teams and gather materials. After about three minutes you notice most students chatting away about subjects unrelated to the project. You say: *"If you can hear my voice, raise your hand."* (Pause with hand raised.) (Softer voice this time.) *"If you can hear my voice, turn your chair this direction."* (Pause and smile.) *"Thank you. I noticed you gathered into trios and got your materials. I also noticed a high level of talking about things other than the water cycle. I wonder if you are unsure of the challenge or the directions and if that has caused the high level of talking. What questions need to be*

answered? How can we get focused on our water cycle posters? Please think of a solution to this problem." (Pause) *"Who has an idea?"*

This third principle, Get It and Give Feedback, is crucial to building success and getting the results you intend; especially in the beginning of the school year or with each new semester. Learn to use this third principle so you can give your full attention to higher levels of interactions. For example, in order to focus on higher order thinking skills or the quality of discussions and projects, the routines and procedures must be clearly communicated and monitored when you first introduce them.

Initially, you'll want to give feedback often to ensure proper implementation. Any inconsistency, over time, settles into mediocrity. When students execute the desired procedure, watch and listen carefully. If you notice any deviation from exactly how you had envisioned it, invite them to do it again – this time with greater precision according to the feedback you give them. Your ability to give consistent, specific feedback lays the groundwork for a solid foundation within your learning community. A smooth-running ship makes for a great cruise!

Pause for a moment to consider the orderliness of your classroom atmosphere. Orderliness fosters creativity and learning (Caine and Caine, 1997). You're not looking for rigidity, but orderliness – a sense of structure that delineates the parameters in which creativity can flourish. Focus on your routines and procedures for a moment (turning in papers, getting supplies, entering and exiting your room). Does the class execute them with the level of consistency and efficiency you had envisioned? Take a moment and analyze one of your classroom procedures. If you need to re-teach it, do so using KEG.

b THE SUCCESS MODEL FROM THE FACILITATOR'S VIEWPOINT

Now that you have the outcome in mind, how do you orchestrate or set students up to succeed? You may have considered it your responsibility to make students learn. Don't. The responsibility to learn belongs to the students.

Take a moment to apply KEG to one of your routines. Write out key information for each part of KEG.

Responsibility assumes someone has the ability to make a response. Students choose moment-to-moment whether or not to learn what you're teaching.

Now, what part do you play? Consider yourself 100 percent accountable for the design and orchestration of learning so that it becomes engaging, enticing, intriguing, full of wonder and discovery. By doing so, you increase the possibility that students will choose to succeed.

How do you orchestrate or set up students to succeed? To ensure student success at the moment of initial learning, reconsider the components you learned in Chapter 5:

- multi-sensory/multi-intelligent first exposure
- chunking and
- frequent review.

We'll now include, from the facilitator's viewpoint, one more:

- the big picture

These four components act as the steel framework in the bridge of understanding. They support the myriad neural connections and associations needed to maximize the moment of learning. Take a look at each in turn, and as you do, allow yourself to analyze the way you introduce new learning. Feel free to jot down ideas in your learning notebook.

The Big Picture

The brain/mind is able to perceive wholes and parts simultaneously. It actively engages in "meaning-making" by linking new information with prior knowledge while simultaneously sorting the information into locations. (Caine and Caine, 1997).

Paint a broad-stroke view of where you wish to take your lesson, how it relates to what students have done or already know, and how it connects to what's coming in the future. Your presentation might sound something like this: *"Today, let's get a feel for the scope of the information revolution. We'll dissect the reasons behind this revolution, or 'To Know Or Not To Know? That Is The Question.' We'll parallel that to what's happening here in our school with 'What's Knowledge Got To Do With It' (to the tune of 'What's Love*

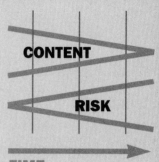

CONTENT

RISK

TIME

Chapter 5
page 86

ENSURE STUDENT SUCCESS AT THE MOMENT OF INITIAL LEARNING

- See the "Big Picture".
- Implement multi-sensory/multi-intelligent first exposure.
- Know that initial learning must be "chunked."
- Use a "frequent review" system.

Got To Do With It?'), *and then we'll take it even further by projecting ourselves into the future, to understand 'The Haves and the Have Nots.'"*

Let this big picture act like a trailer for an upcoming movie. Let it tap into the students' innate feelings of curiosity and wonder. Just highlight the lesson's best parts, and let the learning fill in the plot.

Multi-Sensory/Multi-Intelligent First Exposure

Initial learning must be multi-sensory and multi-intelligent. What does that mean? Simply this: Arrange the learning so that it appeals to students in visual, auditory and kinesthetic ways, while tapping into three or four of your students' multiple intelligences (Armstrong, 1994, Lazear, 1991). Think of a lesson you'll be teaching soon. Imagine how you could use a few of these strategies:

- Capture their interest using an icon of the concept or create an image in their minds.
- Speak in visual, auditory, and kinesthetic predicates as you change your vocal intonation and pace.
- Have students use hand motions to lock the information in their bodies.
- Encourage students to say key words and phrases aloud using a variety of volumes and intonations.
- Create body motions for the key concepts. Then link them together to create dance-like movements.
- Make an acronym with the first letters of each of the steps or concepts.
- Take a nursery rhyme and substitute the words with important facts.
- Display a mural of metaphoric images representing the concepts to be learned.
- Tell a metaphoric story. The characters are the main ideas and their actions and personalities are the details of each main idea.
- Have students brainstorm what they already know about the subject using a mindmap, cluster or other graphic organizer.
- Role-play or mime a scene from the story, or the dynamics of the formula.

Add to this sample list, and let your imagination and creativity run free.

Chunking

Initial learning must be chunked, or organized into palatable sections. Short-term memory allows for the storage and retrieval of seven items plus or minus two (Miller, 1956). Of course, ultimately you want the information to be stored in long-term memory, so first it must enter the short-term. Chunking the information into distinguishable pieces assists the brain in making associations for proper linking and storage. Chunking also provides more opportunities to celebrate.

If It's Worth Learning, It's Worth Celebrating!

Rather than waiting until the students have solved the entire formula, dissected the complete plot, or outlined the whole essay, celebrate the successful completion of the first two steps, the first rise in action, for example, or the opening paragraph constructed. Frequent celebrations build confidence in your learners and amplify their desire to succeed. As we mentioned in Chapter 2, celebrations can take many forms: high fives; placing a star next to the completed portion; verbal affirmations ("I'm learning this quickly") and more.

Chapter 2 page 30

Frequent Review

Employing frequent review builds your learners' confidence with the new concepts. More importantly, the review provides the opportunity to revisit the concept in another way, either visually, auditorially, kinesthetically or through another intelligence. This encodes the new learning by strengthening and building neural pathways. Frequent review also capitalizes on focus and diffusion. (More on this later.) Reviews allow the brain to do something different with the information before it re-focuses.

The Principle of 10-24-7

One way new learning transfers from short-term to long-term memory is through the 10-24-7 principle. Imagine a padlock, like the ones on school lockers. As you focus on the dial notice it has the numbers 1 through 24, with the 10, 24 and 7 highlighted in bright red. A navy blue capital M sits in the middle of the dial, for memory. You just happen to know that the combination for this lock is 10-24-7. As you turn the dial it moves smoothly, clicking at each of the red numbers.

These numbers, 10-24-7 remind you to review initial learning within 10 minutes, within 24 hours and again in 7 days. This time sequence assists in moving information from short-term to long-term memory.

Review strategies you might use include:

- Turn and talk to your neighbor about how mammals care for their young.

- Read over your notes and add a drawing for each stage of cell development.

- Create a series of body motions for this formula.

Again, let your imagination, the modalities and the intelligences guide you in facilitating review strategies.

READING YOUR AUDIENCE

Think about how you felt as you prepared to take your driver's test, or while you sat in one of your methods courses. Now remember one of your favorite teacher's classes. How would you describe your state in each of those situations? And how well did you learn in each class? In your favorite teacher's class we'll bet you learned well. Why? Because all learning is state-dependent. In other words, all learning is embedded in an emotional-physiological condition (Damasio, 1994).

To maximize the moment of learning, orchestrate your learners' states. Assist them in accessing an optimal learning state of relaxed, focused concentration. Your ability to facilitate their state is directly proportional to your students' ability to stay engaged. **State** is comprised of three interwoven components: thoughts, feelings and physiology.

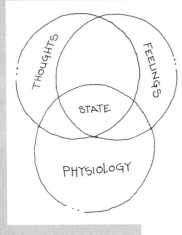

The mind-body connection provides this insight: When we move the body we move the mind, and vice versa. Ever felt like not exercising? Ever felt like not exercising but ended up doing it anyway? What happened? Your mind took control. Ever fallen asleep while reading a textbook? What happened? Your body took control, even though your mind knew you had to finish the text by morning. What our students feel and think manifests itself in their body language. Take boredom, for instance. You know the corresponding body position of that state! Yet with a simple story, intriguing fact, or relevant application of the concept, you entice the students to lean forward – a change in posture that matches a change in thought and feeling.

The implementation of strategies that orchestrate student states for optimal learning is called "state-facilitation." You can accomplish it in a variety of ways. And you can plot each example of state-facilitation along a continuum. On one end are purely physical state-changes (stand and stretch), and on the other end cognitive state-changes ("Imagine this . . ."). You decide what kind of state-changes are most appropriate throughout the lesson.

Check out this list of state-changers (hardly exhaustive!) that we know effectively elicit and maintain an optimal learning state:

- Clap three times.
- Move to a different seat.
- Point your elbow at the ceiling. Point your elbow at me. Keep looking this way and drop your elbow.
- Breathe.
- Be ready when I call on you.
- Think for a moment about how you would answer this question.

Grab a stack of 3x5 cards and create at least 10 state-change cards. Place one state-change on each card. Keep these on or near your desk for easy reference.

d INFLUENCE BEHAVIOR THROUGH ACTION

Ever seen or heard this in a classroom? *"I'm waiting . . . "* (a pause as the teacher looks intently at the clock or watch.) *"It's your recess time you're wasting,"* (another

INFLUENCE BEHAVIOR THROUGH ACTION

- Begin making motions that are tied to the content you're teaching.

- Motion with your hand as if you want them to follow you.

- Write the next direction on the board. Tap the board a few times.

- Responsive clapping: you begin a rhythm and they repeat it.

pause). *"That's fine, I'll stand here until you're ready to learn. We can work through lunch, if that's the way you want it. It's up to you."* Each of those statements accomplishes the same thing. It stops the flow of energy in the room, projects a negative message about learning and erodes the sense of relationship you've been building.

Think of the students' energy in your classroom as a river. As your students engage in learning – interacting in groups, moving from learning center to learning center – the collective energy of the room flows like a river. The energy moves. Stopping the river seems a major undertaking (as in the examples above), but redirecting the river's flow proves to be not only easier but also more elegant.

Influencing **B**ehavior through **A**ction (IBA) captures your learners' attention, and redirects it to the next task or to you. One IBA strategy we use, called *"If you can hear my voice,"* comes in handy when you want to get students' attention as they work in cooperative groups, teams or pairs. Say: *"If you can hear my voice clap once."* Then clap. Repeat the initial phrase, this time inserting *"clap twice."* Then clap twice. As more and more students turn their attention toward you, soften your voice and the sound of the clap. Conclude with, *"If you can hear my voice turn and look this way."* Experiment with this by asking students to snap, tap their fingers on the table/desk, or other movements.

Other ways to influence behavior through action include encouraging students to thank their partners and give their teams applause for their cooperation.

In another situation, you may wish to use this: "Join me when you can." Then begin to do the body motions to a particular dance or to a certain piece of content they've just learned. Say, "Join me when you can" again, this time lowering your voice and starting the motions over again. In less time than it takes to say, "I'm waiting," and the moments that follow, you can have everyone's focus on you by using an Influence Behavior through Action strategy.

Here's a Hot Tip for facilitating short group interactions. Listen for the crescendo. A crescendo is an increase of volume. It works like this. Let's say the task is for students to form trios and formulate a plan of action for their project As students gather in their groups and settle into the tasks, conversations begin. There is a natural rise in volume as ideas are shared, plans discussed, tasks delegated. The volume will peak, and then, if not redirected, will diminish and scatter into off-topic talk. The trick is to listen for the crescendo and just before it peaks, redirect the students focus. For example, you can call for their attention and give the next direction, check in regarding progress, or even request group signs of celebrations for accomplishing the first task.

Call-backs are another effective state-facilitation strategy. They work like this: Make a statement that includes a key word or phrase. Then ask, *"What was that word?"* at which point students respond. Example: *"In the Civil War, an important issue was emancipation. The issue was what?"* Students: *"Emancipation."* When used sparingly, it is a powerful way to "wake up and focus" your learners while bolstering auditory input of key words.

The effectiveness of state-facilitation ties into the concept of focus and diffusion. The brain can focus for a given amount of time and then needs to diffuse that focus. The general formula for this: Age of Brain = Number of Minutes of Focus. Take the age of your students; say it's 14. This equals the number of minutes their brains can focus. After 14 minutes, cement the learning with a one-to-three minute diffusion activity. There are many from which to choose. Consider these:

AGE = FOCUS
Brain   Minutes

- Draw your understanding of imperialism.
- Pretend you are the character in the story. Write a note to a friend about what you're thinking.
- Stand and take a stretch break.

Remember:

Facilitate your students' states and you'll increase their ability to comprehend, participate, focus, and retain information.

Body Motions

Locking the content of your lesson into students' muscle memory facilitates their ability to learn efficiently and recall quickly. Here's how it works: Link the key concepts or steps to hand, arm and/or body motions. For example, the steps for long division are: divide, multiply, subtract and bring down. Hand/body motions could be: Divide – hold left hand horizontal at chest level with right thumb and index finger forming the dots above and below the left hand; Multiply – cross the hands and arms to form an 'x'. Subtract – left hand horizontal at chest level; Bring Down – fists clenched, make a downward motion beginning at chest level.

Nearly everything you teach can be punctuated with a motion. Not only do body motions strengthen the kinesthetic modality and lock the information into muscle memory, they provide another way to get students' attention by influencing their behavior through action.

Special Bulletin:
Take a break!

Breaks

You consciously orchestrate and facilitate everything, even breaks. Offer your students three-to-five minute breaks for every hour of instruction. During these breaks make toys available: soft Frisbees, Nerf balls, hackey sacks, juggling scarves. These activities engage learners in a different way and send a message that learning happens *always*. They also speak of fun and risk-taking. These planned and purposeful breaks interrupt the traditional formats of learning. They refresh the brain and accentuate the moments of attentiveness by allowing the non-conscious mind to integrate the new information.

ELICIT THINKING STRATEGY

Ever wondered why we ask students questions? If you answered anything like what we used to say, you probably said, *"To get an answer!"* Two other purposes come to mind: to dignify students' efforts; and to draw out higher-order thinking skills (HOTS).

First, asking questions gives us the chance to dignify and acknowledge students' participation and risk-taking. Remember, the student is always right. Regardless of the answer the student gives, our job is to discover the matching question, as we discussed in Chapter 2, match the answer. For example: *"What is eight times seven?*

"Fifty-four.

"Thanks for that number. Fifty-four is the answer to nine times six. What is eight times seven?"

Chapter 2 page 29

In this example, you acknowledged the student for his participation, then made it right by finding the question to his answer, and offered another opportunity for him to respond to the initial question. If he doesn't know, tell him you'll get back to him in a moment, and go to another student.

Second, asking questions allows you to elicit and uncover the students' thinking, their progression of thought that leads to the answer given. Example: You ask your class, *"What is the purpose of photosynthesis?"* A student responds, *"To make the plant green."* You could respond, *"Well, that's close. Who could give us the right answer?"* At this point the student feels less than adequate. To probe for more understanding ask, *"That's definitely part of it. Tell me more about what you know."* The student now has the chance to further explain the answer and provide you with a better understanding of her initial answer. You could follow up with, *"What do you know about the meaning of the word photosynthesis based on the two words 'photo' and 'synthesis?'"* After the student responds ask, *"Knowing the definition and also knowing that green is an important component of the process, what can you now say is the definition of photosynthesis?"* The goal is to work with students toward greater understanding of both the concept being studied and of their own thinking behind the concept.

DEBRIEFING MOMENTS OF LEARNING

"Stop and smell the roses," a songwriter wisely suggested. People often offer this advice at times when the tasks of life have eclipsed its rewards. In the classroom, the routines, schedules and curricular demands often overshadow the numerous moments available to enrich the comprehension of the material you teach. You can maximize not only the your students' attentativeness, but also their depth of comprehension. By allowing students time to reflect, you help them establish deeper conceptual understanding, build stronger connections and place greater emphasis on the process of learning.

How can you accomplish this critical task? Make the invisible visible. By eliciting thinking, you make conscious the myriad inter-associations happening in the mind (Caine and Caine, 1997). Once these become conscious, or visible, then greater understanding and stronger connections become possible.

Three questions provide a solid infrastructure for enriching the moment of learning and making the invisible understandings visible.

- What happened?

- What did I learn?

- How can I apply this?

Let's take a look at each question, its intention and possible student responses.

What Happened?

What did you just experience? These questions unlock both the feelings and observable facts. "I felt frustrated. I divided X by 15 and got stuck. I thought I was on the right track." The intention behind this first set of questions is to better understand the student's reality of the situation. By doing so, you'll enter her world, build rapport and gather valuable information regarding her current perceptions.

USE THESE SAMPLE DEBRIEFING QUESTIONS

- Would you please tell us more?

- How does this concept relate to the larger theme of this unit?

- How is what we are studying similar to skateboarding or playing a video game?

- How does your idea relate to what the author says?

- What do you already know about this?

- What is the basic structure?

- What are the hidden and obvious assumptions?

What Did You Learn?

What insights did you have about the process you're working on? What things did you discover based on what you just did? Here, the student might respond, "Well, I learned that I can't divide X by 15. I also discovered I don't quite understand this second step of the equation." Now you've gained a better handle on the distinctions, or lack of distinctions the student has at this point in her learning. You now take the role of coach and provide those distinctions.

How Can You Apply What You've Learned?

How can you use what you just discovered to help you? Here the intention's on whether or not they really understand, and can transfer their understanding to the current situation or to another situation. Give the student time to process this answer. You may need to prompt, give suggestions and pose connections. *"How is what you've learned useful in other areas of your life? What effect would this information have on your ability to solve problems more efficiently?"*

When you weave in questions that invite reflection, students gain a deeper understanding of *why* they should learn the material; they build bridges into other areas of interest; and unearth the

Today I had completely lost control of 32 adolescent students. I was their teacher for the entire day – a day full of learning-how-to-learn skills. Within the first hour my brain began to race. It was obvious I had lost their attention, interest and cooperation. It was time to regroup. Thoughts swarmed about in my head: *"Oh, my. It's only 10:15, and I've lost them. They're talking, messing around and not interested."*

"I don't deserve to be treated this way! (a little ego-stroking, then a long pause.) *What can I do now? What's the most appropriate strategy to use at this time? Come on, Mark, you're a skilled teacher. You have what it takes to pull this group around."* And then a thought that originates only from the heart; a thought that transformed my stuck, confused state into an inspiration. *"Go for it! Tell the truth. Speak to their highest selves."* In they came. On I went.

"Create a poster of the top three tips," I told them. As they meandered into groups and finally settled into the task, I paused, took a breath and scanned. I watched body language. I listened to what they said, and most importantly, I sensed the current situation.

I moved to the front of the class. *"Final minute, everyone."* I reminded myself that the reason I'm in education is because of the potential of human beings. I believe in the softness of adolescents' hearts, and how they desperately want to be called up to their higher selves. I know these guys want to be their best. *"Cap the pens. Please turn your chairs so you can easily and comfortably focus this direction."* I sat on the side edge of the front group's table.

In a sincere voice I shared my thoughts: *"I believe, with all my heart that you really want to be your best. I honestly believe that."* I paused to connect eyes with a few students. *"So the person I'm speaking to right now is the person inside you who chose to be here. Not the person who cops an attitude. Not the person who says, 'This stinks. I don't want to be here.'"* Another pause to connect with a few more students. *"And yet you are here because you chose to be here. For the next few moments I'm speaking to the person who you **really** are. The person that says, 'I want to be my best.'"* A longer pause to let the realness of my message sink in.

The group stayed focused for 45 minutes, engaged in the characterizations of the thinking patterns, bodies still, eyes focused. Speaking to students' highest selves is something they need and crave. No gimmicks. No tricks. Just the "give-it-to-me-straight" stuff.

— Mark Reardon

process of thinking and meaning-making inherent in their learning.

During your next interaction with learners, look for moments to "stop and smell the learning." At first you might only be able to sense these moments in retrospect. Soon, you'll see them coming and design them into your lessons. When the moments arrive, act like a treasure hunter – excitedly patient, eagerly perceptive – unearthing gems of thinking and meaning-making.

REVIEW

You now have elegant strategies to facilitate – make easy – your students' learning. Starting with the outcome in mind, KEG helps to package and deliver your expectations. The Success Model provides guidelines to set students up for increased success. Managing transitions becomes more elegant as you influence behavior through purposeful, content-related motions. Finally, the Elicit Thinking strategy uncovers how students arrive at certain answers and bolsters thinking time.

Of the strategies and ideas you've learned about facilitation, which ones caught your attention? Which ones could you immediately see and/or feel yourself implementing?

Share these with a colleague or friend. As you do, explain in detail when, where and how you'll use each one.

Next, locate a couple of strategies presented in this chapter that you don't yet fully understand. Take a moment to re-read the section containing those ideas. Imagine yourself, in as much detail as you can, successfully implementing those ideas.

Facilitation is the art and science of maximizing the moment of learning by working *with* students – jumping inside their heads and hearts to uncover and explore how they represent and make meaning of what they're learning. It's the part that takes you beyond the dissemination of information to the creation of knowledge and the shaping of lives.

"Stop and Smell the Learning"

R E V I E W

I Know!

Check the box if you know how to:

❏ Communicate expectations using KEG

❏ Facilitate students' success using the four components:

- ▪ Big Picture
- ▪ Multi-Sensory/Multi Intelligent Input
- ▪ Chunking
- ▪ Frequent Review

❏ Unlock the memory padlock using 10-24-7

❏ Influence Behavior through Action

❏ Elicit thinking using a prompt, asking the question, waiting, and eliciting answers

❏ Debrief the moments of learning

Celebrate!

The interactions that facilitate learning!

CELEBRATE

Orchestrating Learning-to-Learn Skills

ENROLL

EXPERIENCE

What if

students learned more in less time, retained more and found school fun and easy?

Imagine . . . Colin smiles
to himself as he notices how
easily he is grasping the new
material. He jots down the key
information in different colors,
creating easy memorization
cues as the teacher presents the
information. He knows that
cementing this new stuff will be
a cinch. His grin widens as he
remembers himself as a student
last year, working way too long
and hard, still not getting it. He
knows that he is a different

student now — actually having fun learning and focusing because he is armed with the skills and strategies of the highest achievers.

How would your life be different if you had a room full of well-organized, highly-focused, eager-to-learn students who came to you armed with:

- Incredible memory and test preparation skills
- Lightning-fast reading speeds
- Tools for more accurate note-taking

On top of all that, what if all your students grasped new material after just one lesson? And they all had the study skills of the highest achievers?

This may read like every teacher's fantasy, but the truth is, with the right study skills, all students can comprehend most information in a shorter amount of time. This would cut down on the amount of time you would need to spend explaining the information. And leave you free to move forward in your curriculum or add extra hands-on enrichment activities.

FIVE SKILLS THAT ELECTRIFY LEARNING

Regardless of the subject matter, students learn faster and more effectively when they master these important skills:

- Focused concentration
- Note-taking
- Organization and test preparation
- Speed reading
- Memorization techniques

As important as these skills are, they've not been part of the traditional school curriculum. Most teachers believe they don't have the time to teach them. They expect students to show up already knowing how to be organized, take notes and study for tests.

a A CASE STUDY: A SCHOOL THAT TEACHES THE FIVE SKILLS

Luckily, we're beginning to see a turnaround. New brain research has pointed the way to better study techniques, and a few pioneering schools have begun to adopt them. In 1994, Peter Anderson, principal of Northwood Middle School

in Woodstock, Illinois, decided to use Quantum Learning methods throughout the entire school, using SuperCamp as a model. To get the most out of it, he decided he needed to go a step beyond training the teachers – and train the students as well.

After being immersed in Quantum Teaching methods and learning-to-learn techniques, and taking the time to co-design classes, the teachers then taught the new skills to the students.

In partnership with Learning Forum, Northwood developed a school-wide program called "SuperStart" to kick off the new school year. It focused on building rapport, teamwork and learning-to-learn skills. During "SuperStart," students learned more effective reading, memory, note-taking and test-preparation skills. Today, Northwood continues to make Quantum Learning skills a part of every class, implemented and supported by the teaching methods outlined in this book. The results have lasted; the entire school continues to enjoy higher test scores and a more positive atmosphere. According to Anderson, "While the atmosphere in the school has historically been positive, this program has taken it to a new level, thanks to the teaching strategies."

By teaching your students how to concentrate, take effective notes, study for exams, increase their reading speed, comprehension and ability to memorize, you're teaching them how to be successful learners. This has effects, both on their academic careers and on the way they see themselves as learners for the rest of their lives.

b TAPPING INTO LEARNING STYLES

Earlier in this book we explained the importance of recognizing visual, auditory and kinesthetic learning styles. Having become familiar with these styles, you now know how to identify and teach to these unique and valuable ways of learning. We'd like to suggest a few ways you can help your students maximize their particular learning styles.

First, explain to them that people learn in different ways, and no one way is better than the others. They each have their strengths. In fact, we all possess all three learning styles; it's just that most often one style dominates (Rose and Nicholl, 1997).

Next, make your students aware of their own learning styles. The following test will help each of them identify his or her style.

RESULTS
After only a few weeks, the results showed marked improvements:

- 8th Grade Language Arts and Reading: Student scores moved from 60 percent of the class receiving B's and A's to 81 percent.

- Social Studies: After one week of Quantum Learning techniques, vocabulary scores increased 13.8 percent and word definition scores increased 11.5 percent.

- Learning Disabled 8th Graders: Out of 28 students, they recorded 17 A's, only 1 D and no F's.

- End of Quarter: The school recorded the lowest number ever of students achieving below C level. The usual number? 30 to 40 out of 170. With Quantum Learning, they had only 10.

(From Northwood Middle School Case Study)

DEMONSTRATE

VISUAL – AUDITORY – KINESTHETIC (V-A-K) ASSESSMENT

Mark the appropriate box for each question. Tally your score for each section. Then graph your results.

VISUAL

	often	sometimes	seldom
■ Are you neat and orderly?	❑	❑	❑
■ Do you speak quickly?	❑	❑	❑
■ Are you a good long-range planner and organizer?	❑	❑	❑
■ Are you a good speller and can you actually see the words in your mind?	❑	❑	❑
■ Do you remember what was seen rather than heard?	❑	❑	❑
■ Do you memorize by visual association?	❑	❑	❑
■ Do you have trouble remembering verbal instructions unless they are written down and do you often ask people to repeat themselves?	❑	❑	❑
■ Would you rather read than be read to?	❑	❑	❑
■ Do you doodle during phone conversations/ staff meetings?	❑	❑	❑
■ Would you rather do a demonstration than make a speech?	❑	❑	❑
■ Do you like art more than music?	❑	❑	❑
■ Do you know what to say but can't think of the right words?	❑	❑	❑

Subtotals _____ _____ _____

x 2   x 1   x 0

Totals _____ + _____ +_____

= _____

AUDITORY

	often	sometimes	seldom
■ Do you talk to yourself while working?	❑	❑	❑
■ Are you easily distracted by noise?	❑	❑	❑
■ Do you move your lips/pronounce the words as you read?	❑	❑	❑
■ Do you enjoy reading aloud and listening?	❑	❑	❑
■ Can you repeat back and mimic tone, pitch and timbre?	❑	❑	❑
■ Do you find writing difficult but are better at telling?	❑	❑	❑
■ Do you speak in rhythmic patterns?	❑	❑	❑
■ Do you think you're an eloquent speaker?	❑	❑	❑
■ Do you like music more than art?	❑	❑	❑
■ Do you learn by listening and remember what was discussed rather than seen?	❑	❑	❑

	often	sometimes	seldom
■ Are you talkative, love discussion and go into lengthy descriptions?	❏	❏	❏
■ Can you spell better out loud than in writing?	❏	❏	❏

Subtotals _____ _____ _____
              x 2   x 1   x 0

Totals _____ + _____ + _____

= _____

	often	sometimes	seldom
KINESTHETIC			
■ Do you speak slowly?	❏	❏	❏
■ Do you touch people to get their attention?	❏	❏	❏
■ Do you stand close when talking to someone?	❏	❏	❏
■ Are you physically oriented and move a lot?	❏	❏	❏
■ Do you learn by manipulating and doing?	❏	❏	❏
■ Do you memorize by walking and seeing?	❏	❏	❏
■ Do you use a finger as a pointer when reading?	❏	❏	❏
■ Do you gesture a lot?	❏	❏	❏
■ Do you have difficulty sitting still for long periods?	❏	❏	❏
■ Do you make decisions based on your feelings?	❏	❏	❏
■ Do you tap your pen, fingers or foot while listening?	❏	❏	❏
■ Do you spend time playing sports and physical activities?	❏	❏	❏

Subtotals _____ _____ _____
              x 2   x 1   x 0

Totals _____ + _____ + _____

= _____

24
23
22
21
20
19
18
17
16
15
14
13
12
11
10
9
8
7
6
5
4
3
2
1
   V   A   K

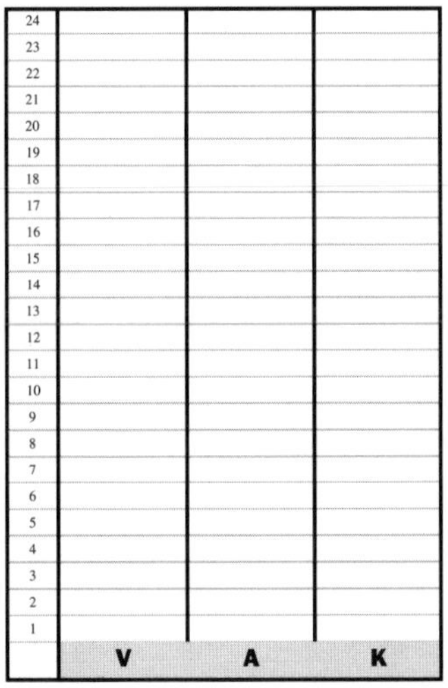

Fill in the graph with your score

Once you've administered the test and your students have identified their learning styles, give them these tips:

Visual Learners

Encourage your visual learners to make lots of symbols and pictures in their notes. In math and science, charts and graphs will further their understanding. Mind Maps can also be excellent tools for Visuals to use in any subject. Since Visuals learn best when they start out with the "big picture," getting an overview of material is extremely helpful. Scanning, for example, gives them an overview of reading materials before they delve into the details.

Auditory Learners

Listening to lectures, examples and stories and repeating information are prime ways for them to learn. Auditories may prefer tape recorders to note-taking, since they like to hear information over and over again. They may themselves repeat out loud what you just said. They were listening, they just like to hear it again. If you find them struggling with a concept, help them talk themselves through it. You can make long strings of facts easy for these students to remember by turning them into a song, sung to the tune of a well-known melody. Some Auditories like to listen to music while they study, others find it distracting. Auditory learners should be allowed to talk quietly to themselves as they work.

Kinesthetic Learners

These learners like lots of hands-on projects. Skits can also prove helpful. Kinesthetics like to learn through movement, and can memorize information best by associating a movement to each fact. Show them how. Many Kinesthetics shun desks; they prefer to sit on the floor and spread their work out all around them.

Encourage your students to adopt all these methods in their learning. You may also want to let parents know what type of learner their child is and teach them the strategies that support that style of learning.

C POWERFUL STATES FOR LEARNING

We learn best when we focus our minds on one thing at a time. Yet we often think of a dozen things at once. While attempting to read or write a paper, the typical student also thinks about how to get a passing grade, worries about completing the assignment, or daydreams about going out with friends. Numerous distractions make concentration difficult, from television and radio, to overheard conversations, to phone calls in the next room. They focus on anything and everything . . . except their assignment.

Most students need to learn how to concentrate. Studies show that students in a state of focused concentration learn faster and more easily. Plus they retain information longer. In other words, they maximize the moment of learning. Teach them to access the best state for learning, and they will learn more, in less time, with less effort.

"State" is a combination of thoughts, feelings and posture. Each state from upset to relaxed, from boredom to excitement, has its own unique combination of these elements. You can access any state you want just by adopting the right combination. Here's what we mean:

In Chapter 6, you did this experiment: Slouch down in your chair and look at the floor. Take deep, slow breaths. This time tell yourself, "This is boring." Do this for a moment. How do you feel? You're experiencing the state of boredom. Now sit up straight. Look up, just above straight ahead. Think to yourself, "This is fascinating!" Hold that thought for a moment. Now you're experiencing the state called interest.

In a matter of a few moments, you changed your state. You are in control. The state you choose has an impact on the results you get in life, in and out of the classroom, and it's the same for your students. By teaching your students these next two quick techniques called SLANT and Alpha State, you can give them tools to access the best state for learning.

SLANT

What do your students look like when they sit at their desks listening to you lecture? Do you find the majority slumped in their chairs with their heads resting on the desks? Do some gaze out the window, while others pass notes? Do they seem to do anything but listen to you? This is not the kind of behavior that inspires your best teaching!

But as you look around the room, you'll probably find a few students who really seem to be paying attention. You usually find them seated in the front row, leaning forward slightly and nodding in response as you make an important point. Occasionally, they raise their hands and ask questions. They hang on your every word and in response, you find yourself teaching mainly to them. They're in a receptive and interested state. Wouldn't it be great if all your students would act like them?

Believe it or not, you can teach your students how to pay attention in class by showing them how to manage their own states. Listening and absorbing information is a skill, just like reading and writing. Once your students master the art of paying attention they'll begin absorbing more material and you'll have a more enjoyable teaching experience.

Let's give your students a new SLANT on learning, a strategy adapted from Dr. Ed Ellis (Ellis, 1991). Show them how to **S**it up in their chairs, **L**ean forward, **A**sk questions, **N**od their heads and **T**alk to their teacher. To reinforce this behavior, try role-playing to give your students a clear idea of what it's like to talk to a group of people who don't pay attention to you. You may want to use the following script:

ENROLL

Teacher: *"Think of a hobby or a sport you enjoy – something you do well that you could teach or explain to another person. Maybe you throw a great football pass, bake a delicious double-chocolate cake, or have a clever strategy for winning at video games. Has everyone thought of something?*

Good. Now take a moment to picture yourself going through the steps involved in your hobby or sport." (Give them a few moments to think.)

"*Raise your hand if you would like to come up and share your experience.*" (Choose a volunteer.)

EXPERIENCE

"*Here's how this will work. Jessica, you are the sharer and I am the listener.*" (Sit down at a chair or empty desk in the front row.) "*Now please tell me all about your hobby. Explain it to me as if you were teaching me how to do it.*" (As the student speaks, exhibit any or all of the following behaviors: slump at your desk, stare at the clock, comb your hair, draw pictures, talk to someone near you, read, mimic other behaviors you've observed in your students. Use your best judgment as to how long to let this go on.)

(To student) "*What did it feel like to explain your hobby to me just now?*"

(Turn to the class) "*How much do you think I learned about how to do what Jessica explained?* "*What did my body language communicate?* "*How do you think Jessica felt?*"

(Turn back to the student, sitting up straight and leaning forward slightly in your chair) "*Please explain your hobby again.*" (As student talks, nod your head, ask questions and act animated and interested.)

(To student) "*How did you feel this time? What was it like?*"

(To class) "*Do you think I learned how to do what you were explaining this time?*
"*What did my body language communicate?*
"*What are some of the differences between how I acted this time and last time?*
"*Which time did Jessica do the better job explaining her hobby? Why?*
"*Who made the difference in how she communicated?* "(Elicit "student" or "listener.")

SLANT

Sit up

Lean Forward

Ask Questions

Nod Your Head

Talk to Your Teacher

LABEL

"That's right! The way you listen makes a difference in how interestingly I teach. And I don't want to bore you. So if you show me you're listening, I'll do my best to be animated and interesting!"

"Now let's learn how to listen in a way that can accelerate your ability to learn quickly. I'm going to show you how to copy the way I listened the second time Jessica shared her story. It's called SLANT. The first step is to Sit up." (Write letters on board or flip chart as you go over each one. Demonstrate sitting up.) *"Next, Lean forward, just slightly."* (Demonstrate.) *"This tells me you're interested and also alerts your brain to be curious. It's easy to pay attention when you sit in this position."* (Ask students to model position.)

"The letter 'A' in SLANT stands for Ask questions. Inquiring minds want to know! Asking appropriate questions that would help you to understand the content keeps your mind engaged. A fun question to ask yourself often in class is 'I wonder what's coming next?' What kind of questions should you ask me? Anytime you don't understand something, just ask me to clarify or restate the information. If you don't understand it, chances are you're not the only one.

"The next letter is N-Nod your head. You probably find yourself doing this (nod) *when you talk to your friends; it shows you're listening and empathizing. Well, it works with me, too. Nodding sends a message both to me and to your brain. It says to me, 'I'm with you,' and it says to your brain that you understand what's being taught. When you nod your head, I feel like you're listening and I do a better job teaching. When I say 'Do you agree?' everyone practice nodding. Ready . . . Do you agree? Thanks, I really feel understood now.*

"The last step is Talk to your teacher. Relationships and learning go hand-in-hand. According to the triune brain theory developed by Dr. Paul MacLean, learning happens in the same part of your brain where relation-ships and connections are made (MacLean, 1990). *If you want to maximize your learning, build a relationship with your teacher. You can do this just by taking a few minutes to say hello at the beginning of class, or stay-*

DEMONSTRATE

ing a few minutes after class to ask questions about the assignment, or share something you learned that day. Talk to me – I love it!

"*Let's review quickly together.*" (Demonstrate each step for visual learners, while making corresponding sound for auditory learners. Have class mimic you to reach kinesthetic learners.)

REVIEW

- "*Sit up.*" (Demonstrate, say "up")
- "*Lean forward.*" (Demonstrate, make creaking sound)
- "*Ask questions.*" (Raise hand, say "huh?")
- "*Nod your head.*" (Demonstrate, say "ah ha")
- "*Talk to your teacher.*" (Palms together, open and close hands, making clapping sound)

"*Turn to someone, give them a high five and say, 'SLANT's for me!'*"

CELEBRATE

Occasionally, you may see students slipping back into their old habits. Cue them by telling them to take a breath and adjust their posture. You should also do this whenever you begin a lecture. However, always remind them as their learning coach rather than demand it like a drill sergeant. Make sure you model attentive behavior yourself when your students address you or the class.

hot tip

Students find it easier to pay attention when they sit near or in the front row. To give all your students the benefit of a front row seat, arrange desks in a horseshoe or semi-circle, or switch the seating periodically.

Alpha State

In the mid 1970's, Dr. Georgi Lozanov conducted experiments on the best state for learning. He discovered that students in Alpha State – a condition of relaxed concentration – learn at a much faster rate. They also remember information for longer periods of time (Schuster and Gritton, 1986). Humans exhibit four states of brain wave activity: beta, alpha, theta and delta. In beta, you feel alert and active. Theta is a state of being nearly asleep or dreaming and delta is deep, dreamless sleep.

How can you use this information? You can help your

students become better learners by teaching them to easily access Alpha State whenever they could benefit from focused concentration, such as when they're reading, solving math problems or writing essays.

The first time you teach them to access Alpha, you'll need to walk them through the following visualization. Afterward, they should be able to call up the images quickly on their own. The more often they use this technique, the more adept they'll become at accessing this state.

You can use this script for accessing Alpha State the first time:

Teacher: (Speak slowly in a quiet, relaxed tone.) *"Close your eyes and take a few deep breaths. Feel yourself relaxing. Picture a place where you feel relaxed and at peace. Maybe you're in your bedroom lying down for a few moments after school. Or you might be in your favorite chair in the family room, or at the beach. Imagine the sounds you hear in this place, what it looks like, the touch of things around you."* (Allow a few moments of silence to anchor these thoughts in their minds.)

"Now open your eyes. How did that feel? What are some of the places you pictured? Now let's take a moment to practice visualizing again. Close your eyes and think of this special place again. Feel like you're there." (Do this for just a moment.) *"Open your eyes. Did everyone get there immediately?"* (You may want to practice a few times if needed.)

Using Alpha State

Once your students have learned to access their peaceful place, you won't need to repeat the visualization. Whenever you want your students to really concentrate, just do the following steps developed by educational consultant Steve Snyder.

First, adjust their postures. Tell your students to sit up and lean forward slightly with feet flat on the floor.

Next, have students close their eyes, take a deep breath and think of the special place they visualized, roll their eyes up, then down and then open them. This should only take a moment. When they open their eyes, they should feel focused, relaxed and alert.

One of the benefits of SLANT and Alpha State is that they promote a positive attitude about learning. Instead of feeling stress and worry, students feel relaxed and focused. In a state of focused concentration, learning comes faster and easier. Consequently, they have a more positive attitude about school and greater confidence in their ability to learn.

ACCESS THE ALPHA STATE

- Adjust your posture.

- Close yours eyes and take a deep breath.

- Think of a peaceful place.

- Roll your eyes up, then down, and open them on the subject.

d ORGANIZING INFORMATION

Knowing how to organize information is a valuable skill. Some people seem well organized by nature; most of us, however, are not. Ability to organize depends somewhat on age and learning style.

As a teacher, one of the best things you can do for your students is to give them organizational tools. Mind Mapping, Notes:TM and Circuit Learning are skills they can use in any class, at any grade level. Mind Mapping and Notes:TM help students capture thoughts and ideas on paper in a clear, concise and easy manner. These brain-compatible methods make the information easier to understand and recall, maximizing the moment of learning. Circuit Learning is a test preparation tool that builds on these note-taking methods.

Mind Mapping®

A good note-taking method should help us remember what was said or read, increase our understanding of the material, help us organize the material and provide us with new insights. Mind Mapping makes all of this possible. Developed by Tony Buzan, Chairman of the Brain Foundation, Mind Mapping is a creative note-taking method that makes it easy to remember lots of information. When completed, the notes you made form a pattern of connected ideas, with the main topic in the center and sub-topics and details branching outward. The best Mind Maps are colorful and use lots of pictures and symbols; they often look like a work of art!

This note-taking method, based on research on how the

Use pictures and symbols

brain processes information, works with your brain, rather than against it (Buzan, 1993). Experts once thought the brain processed and stored information linearly, much like the traditional note-taking method. Scientists now know the brain takes information – a jumble of images, sounds, smells, thoughts and feeling – and sorts it into a linear form, such as speech or writing. When the brain recalls information, it often does so in the form of colorful pictures, symbols, sounds and feelings (Damasio, 1994).

Mind Mapping imitates the thinking process in that it allows you to jump from subject to subject. You record information via symbols, pictures, emotional significance and in full color, much the way the brain processes it. And because Mind Mapping engages both sides of the brain, you can recall the information with more ease. Now that you know why it works, we'll show you how it's done.

How to Make a Mind Map

Let's pretend *you* are the student, and you're listening to a lecture on the life of Michelangelo. You want to try out your new Mind Mapping skills. Take out a blank piece of paper and turn it horizontally. In the center of your page, write Michelangelo, your subject.

Your teacher begins the lecture by giving you a brief biography of the artist's life. You draw a thick line extending out from the subject, graduating in thickness, and label it "biography." For each topic the teacher discusses – biography, paintings, sculpture – you draw thick lines reaching out from the center, like spokes on a wheel. You label each line, using a separate color for each topic.

Now your teacher begins to go into more depth on Michelangelo's biography. You draw smaller lines coming out of the topic line, like twigs on a branch. Along each of these smaller lines you write down some facts, like date of birth, birthplace and so on, and make symbols, pictures and other cues to help you remember the information.

Toward the end of the lecture, your teacher backtracks to discuss "paintings." No problem – you simply add another line to your branch. At the end of the lecture, he repeats key facts which you then realize will be on the test. You draw a star next to each of these facts on your Mind Map. You notice he really emphasizes the artist's sculptures, so you decide to shade that area. When the lecture ends, you add detail to a few of your branches, maybe a little more color, and spruce up your symbols. You stand back and admire your colorful creation. (When was the last time you did that with your notes?) You now have a clear, well-organized and memorable Mind Map.

Beyond lectures, students can also use Mind Maps for reading assignments, brainstorming and writing. As soon as they finish a reading assignment, encourage your students to Mind Map what they've just read. This improves both comprehension and recall, and they can use the Mind Map later to study for a test.

Mind Maps also work great for brainstorming sessions, especially when the students work in groups and many people shout out ideas at once. One student can quickly record the information while others continue to discuss the topic. Mind Maps were made for leaps in thought, because they work the way the brain works, actually encouraging insights and bright ideas.

During challenging writing assignments, a Mind Map helps students organize information and get their thoughts going. It can even help them overcome writer's block. A writing assignment or brainstorming session may generate several Mind Maps, as one of the main topics may develop into a new subject with

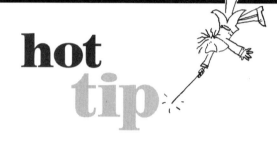

hot tip

- Use a different color for each main topic, or alternate colors.

- Show associations by drawing an arrow between branches.

- Develop your own shorthand of pictures, symbols and abbreviations.

- Put the information in chronological order by numbering the branches.

- Be creative!

further thought and exploration. This doesn't mean you did the original Mind Map wrong or that it had no initial value. The branching off is part of the natural process of exploring ideas and organizing information.

A great way to introduce and reinforce Mind Maps is to use them yourself. As you lecture, draw your own Mind Map on a flip-chart or board, creating Mind Maps in the moment. Handouts and other materials usually created in linear form can also be Mind Mapped.

Most students find Mind Maps a fun, interesting way to take notes. At first, some may hesitate to use this new method for fear they'll miss information. It takes a little practice to get comfortable with it, but encourage them to continue and the rewards will be great.

Notes:TM

Ever catch your students daydreaming in the middle of an important lecture? Here's why: You speak at a rate of 200 to 300 words per minute. The brain can process language at 600 to 800 words per minute. During long lectures, your students' minds start to fill in that lag time with "more interesting" things: tomorrow's date, last Friday's football game, today's lunch. Your words trigger associations that send your students off to la-la land.

A variation of Cornell Notes, we developed Notes:TM so that your students can use their incredible daydreaming abilities to focus on the task at hand.

Notes:TM stands for Notes: Taking and Making. Your students record both the facts from your lecture and the associations, thoughts and feelings that sent them on their mental journey. Writing these thoughts down helps them become more aware of them, which makes it easier to keep their focus on you. Recording the associations that correspond with the information you teach also improves retention; information linked to emotions is easier to recall.

How It's Done

Notes:TM is easy to learn and very effective. Your students will need a piece of notebook paper, two colored pens or pencils and a highlighter. Have them draw a vertical line about one quarter of the way in from the right edge of the paper, forming two columns, one large and one small. At the top of the larger left-hand column, they write "Important Information." At the top of the smaller right-hand column, they write "Thoughts, feelings and questions." The left-hand column is the note-taking area; the smaller, right side is the note-making area.

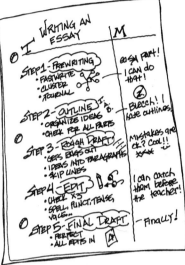

On the left side, it's business as usual, with students writing down important dates, names and other information while listening to a lecture, reading text or watching a film. Whenever you switch points or topics, your students switch colors. The brain likes distinctions, and this helps students distinguish between the different types of information when they look at their notes.

On the right side, they write down any associated thoughts that pop into their heads. These can be opinions, reactions to what they heard, questions, whatever. They might even find it helpful to draw pictures and symbols in this area. This right side is also used to write down their feelings at that moment – sad, interested, confused, bored and so on. By doing so, they create an emotional relationship to the information they are learning, which helps it stick in their minds. This means faster learning for them and less time repeating and reviewing for you.

Now for the final step: This one can really make a difference in their grades. At the end of the lecture, give your students about 90 seconds to quickly review their notes. They then distinguish important facts by highlighting them and adding exclamation marks, circling vocabulary words and starring test material. Again, these distinctions help the brain retain information more effectively. You can develop a system of symbols for the whole class to use, or let the students come up with their own system.

When it comes time to study for an exam, the students need only look over the highlighted portions, picking out the appropriate symbols. As you well know, anything that makes studying faster and easier is welcomed by students. The distinctions – the different colors and symbols – make the information more memorable. In the note-making area, recalling the feelings and associations they experienced at the moment of learning also makes the information easier to recall.

Circuit Learning

You now have the ability to teach powerful states for learning and two highly effective note-taking methods. Now we'll put them all together for a new test preparation tool, Circuit Learning. We call this method "Circuit" Learning because students actually run through the information in the same pattern every day, like electricity running through the circuits of a house. John LeTellier, a Quantum Teaching facilitator and educational consultant, developed this method. It's a real time-saver, and only takes about 10 minutes a day. By maximizing class time, you minimize study time.

Circuit Learning starts with a confident, successful state of mind. Most students have a negative association with tests. They get scared, and the fear causes them to shut down. After hours of studying, they draw a blank when they see the test in front of them. Even the most diligent students sometimes have trouble taking tests. So the first step is to break through that negative state and replace it with empowering thoughts and feelings. The following visualization and affirmations can help.

Here's a script for Success Images:

Teacher: *"Everyone take a deep breath, hold it, now exhale. Close your eyes. Now think of a time when you did well on a test or quiz – a time when you felt really proud of your achievement. Picture that classroom, the teacher, your desk, the subject. Feel the sensations of success – confidence, joy, pride, accomplishment. Allow yourself to be in that moment. Now take another deep breath, and slowly exhale.*

"Now open your eyes. With those feelings of

success still inside you, please write down a short statement or affirmation about your test-taking abilities. It might be something as simple as: 'Come on, gimme that test!'"

Once students have written down their affirmations, invite them to share what they've written. Teacher: *"Now that you've discovered a new approach to test-taking, let's put it to practice. You remember Alpha State. Now we're creating a new test-taking state. Everyone please stand up. Stand tall, confident, shoulders back. When I say the word 'test,' shout out the statement you just wrote down. Ready, TEST!"*

You may also want to role-play handing out tests using blank sheets of paper, and ask students to shout out affirmations or say them quietly to themselves. Once your students have the attitude down, it's time to teach the technique of Circuit Learning.

Let's say it's Monday morning, and you announce to your students they'll be learning about William Shakespeare and briefly exploring some of his work. You plan to give a biography of Shakespeare on Monday, read scenes from "Romeo and Juliet" on Tuesday, "Hamlet" on Wednesday, "The Merchant of Venice" on Thursday and selected sonnets on Friday. You plan to give a test on the following Monday.

M	T	W	T	F	S
begin MM	review & add to MM	review & add to MM	review & add to MM	review & add to MM	review MM
					S
					rest
					M
					Test!

That evening, your students begin a Mind Map on the week's topic, using their notes from class. For example, they make one branch for Monday labeled "biography" and fill in the information. They leave enough room to continue filling in further information throughout the week.

On Tuesday, students review Monday's information. Then they add another branch, "Romeo and Juliet" and fill in that information. On Wednesday, they review previous learning from Monday and Tuesday, and add another branch, "Hamlet." Throughout the week, they continue with this pattern – add and review, add and review.

The whole process takes only a few minutes each day. (Make sure you emphasize this to your students.) Since they're copying the information from class notes either in

hot tip

Encourage students to put a question mark next to anything they didn't understand. After class, they can ask you to clarify the information.

Notes:TM or Mind Map form, it should take only a few minutes to pick out key information to record on the week's Mind Map. Reviewing takes only about two minutes, so the most time they would ever spend on studying these notes would be just ten minutes! And even this amount of time would happen only at the end of the week, when they've completed their Mind Map.

Now for Saturday and Sunday. On Saturday, they review the completed Mind Map – again, about ten minutes of their time. Now here comes the exciting part: On Sunday, they recreate the Mind Map from memory, including the original Mind Map's colors, word placement and symbols. This activity really helps cement the information in their minds. When they've completed their Mind Map, they can compare it to the original to see how much information they got right and what they need to focus on.

This is one of the easiest and fastest test preparation tools you'll find. Since it takes so little time, it's perfect for students juggling several exams in their schedule – even if they have them all on the same day. As we mentioned before, this method works because it capitalizes on note-taking methods that help students maximize the moment of learning.

e TAPPING CREATIVE GENIUS

Quantum Reading

How would you like all of your students to get their reading assignments done on time, with greater comprehension? As you know, reading well is a valuable skill that you use throughout life. Yet many students find reading a chore. Some put off reading until the last minute, then find they don't have time to complete the assignment. In the upper grades, students may have reading assignments from several classes due at once – a daunting task for even the best readers. If reading were fast and easy, students would be more likely to complete their work. And if their comprehension increased, they'd get higher grades and complete their studying in less time. School would be easier. Life would be easier. College would be a reality just around the corner. Once they experienced easy, successful reading, they might even begin to read more often – not just for school, but for pleasure. Quantum Reading can truly open many doors.

Here's how it works: Your brain wants to read quickly. It can comprehend many more words than you usually feed it at the average reading rate. But what happens when you face a difficult reading assignment? If you're like most of us, you slow down, thinking the slower you read, the more you'll understand. Ironically, the opposite occurs; reading slowly causes boredom, and your mind starts to wander. Before you know it, you've finished a paragraph without having any idea what you've just read.

Using a combination of high interest level, highly focused concentration and specific reading strategies, Quantum Reading capitalizes on the brain's ability to grasp several words at once. You can put it into practice in five easy steps.

1. Be A Curious Learner

Quantum Reading means asking questions. Before you begin each reading assignment, ask yourself:

- What is this about?
- What do I want to get out of this?
- How can I use this information?"

Up the interest level by giving yourself a reason to want to read. Remember: Inquiring minds want to know.

2. Get into a State of Focused Concentration

Fast reading demands high concentration. Have your book propped up on your desk. Use Alpha State to read your best. To access alpha, sit up; close your eyes and take a deep breath; think of your peaceful place (from the earlier exercise); roll eyes up and down; open your eyes and look at your book.

3. SuperScan

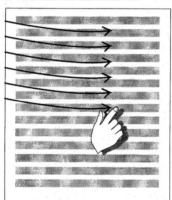

Once in Alpha, begin to SuperScan your book. This is your fastest reading. Quickly go through each page of your reading assignment. See the whole page at once. Let your finger "ski" down the page in a back and forth motion, like a skier slaloming down the slopes, pulling your eyes down the page quickly. Let your eyes follow your finger, looking for anything that stands out – chapter headings, bold type, pictures, graphs, questions at end of the chapter. Do this several times to get familiar with the material so you have some idea what the book is about; then when you begin reading, you'll read faster and understand more.

As you scan, keep asking yourself, "I wonder what that's about? What does that mean? Why is this person important?" Your mind loves questions and automatically searches for answers. When you go back and read the material, the answers pop out at you.

4. Read

Again, get into Alpha State. As you begin reading, follow the type with your finger line-by-line, just as you did when you first learned to read. Push yourself to read a little faster than comfortable. You can double your reading speed just by using your finger as a visual guide. As your finger pushes your eyes across the page, you read faster and more efficiently than before. Your finger keeps you from losing your place and backtracking over the same words.

Many of us read one word at a time. The left brain emphasizes this focus on parts. Our goal as Quantum Readers is to read whole groups of words at once using the right brain, the part that understands the whole group. As you move your finger along, see several words together; phrases have greater meaning than individual words.

5. Review

Mind Map what you've just read. This cements the

learning in your memory and increases your understanding of the material. Later you can use the Mind Map to review for a test.

Auditory learners benefit from talking about what they've just read. Encourage them to explain what they've read to another student, or talk to themselves about their reading.

Using the methods outlined above, most students can significantly increase their reading speed and comprehension; at SuperCamp, many scores more than double. If you really want to dazzle your students with their new reading speeds, we suggest a pre-test and post-test to measure their improvement. To do this, you'll need a stopwatch and a section of reading material.

Give your students exactly one minute to read the assignment, using your stopwatch as a timer. At the end of one minute, say "Stop" and tell your students to mark the last line they read. Then have 10 questions prepared for them to answer immediately upon completing the reading. Have the students count the number of lines read and multiply that number by the average number of words per line. That answer equals their reading speed.

After practicing Quantum Reading a few times, repeat the test. Most students see a vast improvement. It's exciting to see what they've accomplished, and they're more likely to use Quantum Reading when they see for themselves that it really works.

We suggest walking your students through the Quantum Reading steps whenever you give a reading assignment. It takes only about five minutes, and the review makes a habit of the process.

After a reading assignment, pair students up and let them take turns explaining the material to each other. This improves comprehension and memory, and anything they don't understand suddenly becomes apparent. Save time for questions!

Maximizing Memory

Your mind stores everything you've seen, heard or felt. That means you have a perfect memory. The challenge is recalling the information. You can help your students (and yourself) remember long lists of places, names, dates and other information with a few simple memory techniques.

Special Bulletin:
Memory is the art of attention

To have a good memory you must consciously input not only facts, but also meaning and associations. If information has meaning to you, you'll remember it much easier than you will a list of random facts and figures. To maximize memory, you must make information meaningful.

By meaningful, we mean both understanding the information well and giving it personal meaning. Often, students don't recall information for tests because it has little meaning to them; it's all just a jumble of names and dates. Knowing what makes this information important goes a long way toward helping students remember it. Giving it personal meaning – associating it with things in their own lives – also helps.

Building on that, making vivid associations is an incredible tool, limited only by your imagination. Recent brain research shows that linking information to strong sensory perceptions – sight, sound, smell, taste and feel – makes it much easier to recall because the brain organizes information into these categories, storing bits of information separately. When you think of a rose, for example, you recall from different parts of the brain the color, smell, and feel of the flower. But the pieces all come together to form a rose (Damasio, 1994).

By exaggerating sensory images, you can come up with truly memorable ways to remember. Crazy sights and bright colors, exaggerated sounds, pungent odors, the feel of things, even strong emotions, all help us recall information easily. Here's an example:

Let's say you want your students to remember that Wolfgang Amadeus Mozart composed "The Marriage of Figaro." You might tell them to think of a man named Mo holding up a huge colorful painting (Mo's art, for Mozart). In this painting, a bride and groom stand amidst a row of fig trees. The figs hang in a row above the couple. Loud music plays, and Mo sings at the top of his lungs, "Figaro, Figaro, Figaro!"

Most students have fun with this. When teaching memory, give them examples like the one above, then let them make up their own associations. The more outrageous you make it, the more likely they are to remember. You may want to make a game of it; give them the association first, then let them guess what you're teaching. We use this method a lot at SuperCamp. It keeps the students on the edges of their seats, waiting to discover what they'll learn. Experiencing the sudden "Aha!" or the pop of figuring it out makes it fun and memorable.

Linking/Storying

Use the linking method to teach long lists of information, especially when you want that information memorized in a specific order. Using association, link each item to the next, like the links in a chain.

As an example, let's say you want to teach your students the following information about how the heart pumps blood.

Heart function: The heart contains four chambers; the right and left atria and the right and left ventricles. One-way valves control the flow of blood through these four chambers. Blood traveling to the heart from various body parts is bluish. It turns red when mixed with oxygen. Blood from the body first flows into the right atrium, then down to the right ventricle. The heart then pumps it to the lungs. There, the blood exchanges carbon dioxide, a waste product, for oxygen.

Oxygenated blood flows to the left atrium. It then flows to the left ventricle, which pumps the blood away from the heart to the rest of the body via the aorta, the main artery. Link that information through a story such as this:

> *Upon arrival at the famed Heart Hotel,*
> *you order a tour of the facilities. Your*

chambermaid, Blood Flow, promptly arrives to conduct the tour. She tells you the Heart Hotel has four chambers – two atriums and two vents. She first takes you into the right atrium. You look around and notice all the plants are blue. Blood Flow has also turned blue. You want to turn back, but the valve on the door won't open from this side – you and Blood Flow can only go one way. Not only that, but from this atrium, you can only go through a vent to move on. You continue on, crawling through the vent to the right. You hear a sound: 'trickle, trickle, trickle.'

"The right vent trickles," your guide explains. You come out in a room with two large pumps marked 'L-lungs.' Blood Flow exchanges a filled garbage bag marked 'CD-carbon dioxide' for a shiny new bag marked 'O-oxygen.' As she takes the oxygen, she turns bright red. She then takes you through another door on the left, marked Atrium. In the left atrium, all the plants are red. You then crawl through the left vent, and again hear 'trickle, trickle, trickle.'

"The left vent trickles," Blood Flow says again. When you emerge from the vent, she pushes you out and says, 'Come again.' In a hoarse voice you answer 'I otta' (Aorta)."

Location Method

With this method, we associate the information we wish to remember with specific locations. We can recall information easily if we put it in a specific place, see it there, and give it sound and action. The wilder your associations, the easier they are to remember.

Your students can use any place or thing familiar to them. Just tell them to make sure to use something they can easily picture in their minds, like parts of the body, a clock face or the classroom seating arrangement, for example. For each item they learn, they should come up with a corresponding location, movement and sound.

Let's say your class needs to memorize five vocabulary words for Friday's quiz. You really want everyone to ace the

test and feel successful, so you teach them the
following method:

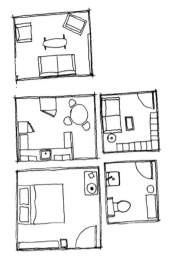

Teacher: *"Imagine five rooms in your home. We
will hang one vocabulary word on each point,
including the word's definition. Let's start at the
top and work clockwise.*

*"Everyone picture your home and locations in it. It
has five rooms. Balanced on the top of the door are
two old-fashioned dueling pistols. You hear the
loud bang! as they fire at each other."* (Point your
fingers like imaginary guns shooting at each other.)
*"They continue shooting until both pistols split into
two parts.*

"First word: Dualism.

*"Definition: the state of being dual or having
two parts.*

*"Now, on the coffee table in your home is a crystal
ball. With it you can see the future. Say 'ooooo.'"*
(Wave hand across imaginary crystal ball.) *"As you
wave your hand across it, a large number four
appears. You watch as the four begins to hunch
over, until it becomes very bowed.*

"Second word: Forebode

"Definition: To foretell or predict.

*"On the dining table is a big jar of a new miracle
skin cream. The lid says 'Inva,' the name of the
cream. A thin, sickly woman tries to screw off the
lid and apply the cream, but she is so sickly she
cannot take care of herself."* (Pretend to struggle
with opening a jar. Make loud grunting noises.)

"Third word: Invalid

*"Definition: A sickly person, unable to care
for self.*

*"In the kitchen, unsophisticated Eve sits holding an
apple. But when the serpent tells her to eat the
apple, she says 'Nah, nah, I won't do it this time.'"*

(Shake your head.)

"Fourth word: Naive

"Definition: Simple, unaffected, unsophisticated.

"In the bedroom you see a huge vacuum cleaner called the Prag-O-Matic. For a very practical price, it can do all your cleaning – carpets, drapes, upholstery, you name it. It runs on solar energy, very practical. It makes a loud humming noise." (Demonstrate, and pretend to push it, like a large vacuum.)

"Fifth word: Pragmatic

"Definition: Concerned with practical considerations; a practical point of view."

Most students have a lot of fun with the memory skills. They enjoy using their imaginations to come up with outrageous associations and they like showing off their incredible memories. Reinforce the skills by using them in class from time to time, and remind students to use them at home when studying for tests.

Once your students get a handle on memorization, we suggest making a game out of it. Teach the associations first, as if telling a story. Then, let the students try to figure out what they just learned. It makes learning fun and keeps them on the edges of their seats.

REVIEW

Imagine now, students who want to learn and have the skills to learn effectively. Knowing their learning style, they grasp material in a way that works best for them. They organize material efficiently using Mind Mapping, Notes:TM and Circuit Learning. Your students are becoming Quantum Readers as they tap into Alpha State and memorize important information with fun, meaningful associations. What a joy to teach to a classroom full of these students.

I Know!

Check the box if you know how to empower your students with these skills:

- ❏ Personal Learning Style
- ❏ Powerful states for learning
- ❏ Mind Mapping and Notes:TM
- ❏ Quantum Reading
- ❏ Memory Techniques

 *Your students' ability to take charge of their learning!*

CELEBRATE

Orchestrating Life Skills

ENROLL

What if

your classroom was a place where students modeled the 8 Keys, communicated clearly, took responsibility for their actions and cleaned up broken agreements easily?

What effect would this kind of interaction have on your teaching?

Imagine . . . *Colin feels himself get irritated by his classmate's antics. A fleeting temptation to say something rude passes, as he looks around the room at the 8 Keys on the walls. He checks in with himself on Ownership – What does HE have to do with this frustrating situation? He knows it isn't really all his classmate's fault. He also checks his own Speaking With Good Purpose – What else could he say to handle the situation smoothly and just move on? He takes a deep breath, quickly uses one of the simple communication models he learned in this very class and resolves the issue with his neighbor. They both get right back to their work at hand, tension gone.*

EXPERIENCE

Just as any masterful conductor brings out the beautiful music within each of his musicians, you orchestrate your students' authenticity and efficacy through personal skills. Otherwise known as "life skills" or "social skills," these abilities empower each of us to build and maintain rapport and relationship with others – yet we never learn them in school. Not having these skills handicaps students in their lives, and it seems the "at-risk" students are often the ones who lack them.

Ronald Brandt, former editor of *Educational Leadership* notes, "Parents are sending us the best kids they have. They're not leaving the good ones at home!" Brandt reminds us that we get students as they are regardless of how much we wish their parents – or at least last year's teacher – had done a better job with them.

As Judith Anderson, lecturer at Columbia Business School attests, many corporations list "personal skills" as the number one attribute missing in graduates from top business schools. Companies say that "the cream of the crop" in business schools do well in school, but not in life. They can strategize and defend on paper, but can't think on their feet. They're good at competing, but not at cooperating. The strategies that worked to get them to the top of their classes throughout their educational life prove less than effective in the reality of the work world.

These strategies include:

- competing,
- following the guidelines,
- doing as they're told without questioning (compliance),
- keeping answers and great ideas to themselves,
- doing their own work,
- believing the answer is either right or wrong and
- thinking negative feedback means failure.

In real life, negative feedback doesn't mean failure – or anything else. It has no intrinsic meaning. It's just a message that says, "Try again."

At SuperCamp, we've had great success helping students develop these life skills. Students gain confidence, learn self-expression and feel excitement about the possibilities of who they are (Vos-Groendendal, 1991).

Of SuperCamp graduates:

- 81% develop more confidence,
- 84% increase self-esteem,
- 80% have better relationships and
- 90% improve self-image.

You can achieve the same with your students, in your classroom! By going beyond content, you can equip them to be more effective in their lives.

LABEL

For example, think back to the 8 Keys of Excellence in Chapter 3. As part of the Foundation, the Keys provide the backdrop for all of your teaching, learning and personal interaction. They also make a significant difference in students' lives. As you weave them into your content, and consistently model them, they become a way of being – the threads that hold the tapestry of your classroom together – not just nice ideas.

Chapter 3
page 48

ⓐ LIVING ABOVE THE LINE

Wouldn't you like it if all your students came from a place of such responsibility in their every action that when certain classmates avoided responsibility the others would call them on their actions? You can orchestrate that environment! "Living Above the Line," a powerful life skill, comes not from education, but from Money & You, a course for entrepreneurs and business people. As a foundation for communication and personal interaction, Living Above the Line highlights and puts into practice one of the 8 Keys, Ownership, taking responsibility for one's actions. This Key alone has positively influenced many businesses and Quantum Teaching environments.

Share this skill with your students, especially in the first few days of class. Use the diagram to the right as a reference cue for all of you (everyone in the learning community, teachers and students alike). Post it on your classroom wall. Within days, you'll find students holding each other accountable for their level of Ownership –
taking responsibility for their words and actions.

Basically, you can live two ways: Above the Line or Below the Line. Here's what we mean:

LIVING "ABOVE THE LINE"

Accountability   Choices

Solutions   Freedom

Willingness

RESPONSIBILITY

Laying Blame

Giving Up   Justifying

Reasons   Denying

LIVING "BELOW THE LINE"

Living Below the Line

Some people use Below the Line characteristics like laying blame, justifying, denying and quitting as handy alternatives to responsibility.

Laying Blame

The easiest and perhaps the most damaging form of Below the Line thinking.

> **Teacher Example**
>
> *The principal called a special meeting after school yesterday and instructed us to work on his special project instead of our grading last night.*

> **Student Example**
>
> *She was talking to ME – I wasn't talking.* While you may think you have a viable excuse, it doesn't solve the problem or promote responsibility, and it's sure to cause bad feelings.

Justifying

Coming up with a reason why you didn't perform as expected.

> **Teacher Example**
>
> *I had so much other work to do last night, I couldn't get to your papers.*

> **Student Example**
>
> *Everyone else is talking too.*

This Below the Line thinking tries to provide reasons for failure, believing that the reason or excuse will make everything okay.

Denying

This doesn't make the problem go away.

> **Teacher Example**
>
> *What papers? I never said I'd have those done today.*

> **Student Example**
>
> *I wasn't talking.*

These obviously ineffective responses can cause others lots of frustration, and make you seem unreliable or dishonest.

Quitting (Giving Up)

The most disheartening form of Below the Line thinking. When you believe so strongly that you'll fail that you don't even bother to try, you sabotage your chances for success even before you've begun. That kind of thinking gives you an excuse for your failure. You deceive and diminish yourself when you respond this way.

Teacher Example
> *I knew I couldn't get them done, so I didn't even try. It's not important anyway.*

Student Example
> *Yeah, whatever.*

Living Above the Line

Above the Line sits response-ability, which we define as "having the ability to respond." With this ability come choices and freedom. Living Above the Line means being accountable for your actions and willing to make correction when necessary. It means looking at your options, choosing solutions and finding ways to become more effective. Above the Line thinking leads to greater freedom. You're not just sitting back and accepting failure; you're using your experiences to move you toward success. Rather than being controlled by circumstances, you determine your own actions.

> *"Response-ability"*

Example
If you don't get graded papers back to your students when you promised them AND you're living Above the Line, you might say to the class:

> *"I haven't completed your papers, and I apologize. What can I do to make it right? How about I give you an extra day to turn in today's homework, or we have a free homework day? I'll do my best to have future papers back to you on time."*

For students living Above the Line, the message may sound like this: If you ask a student to stop talking in class, she says, "Okay," and stops talking.

When you play Above the Line, you take responsibility for your life. You begin to make things happen. You have greater control because you stop blaming things outside yourself for your current situation. This is a major AHA! for many students. They can take Ownership of their education, relationships or other areas of their lives. They can create a huge shift in their lives simply by taking Ownership of their attitudes.

Taking Ownership also means not blaming others for what happens to you. Blaming your parents, social status or circumstances only leads to dead ends. Response-ability is the ability to respond to what happens to you, rather than just accepting it. When you sit back and accept, things happen to you. When you take action, you make things happen.

b CLEAR COMMUNICATION: VISIBLE VS. INVISIBLE

What if you and your students had some easy, effective language for handling conflict and human error? How could the learning and relationships in your class be enhanced? From what you've read in this book, you know how important it is to model clarity in communication with students, especially in emotionally-charged situations. The first step toward achieving this clarity is to be sure the communication is **visible** rather than **invisible**. Allow us to demonstrate.

Imagine your best friend phones you right now and asks, *"What are you doing this Friday night?"*

You could answer, *"I'm busy."* To which your friend could respond, *"That's too bad. I've got two tickets to see your favorite musician this Friday night. But that's ok. I can ask someone else."*

What would you think? Probably, *"Whoa, if I'd known, I might have given a different answer!"*

Then again, you could answer, *"I'm not doing anything this Friday night,"* to which your friend might respond, *"Great! I have two tickets to your favorite musician and I'd love it if you could baby-sit so I can go to the concert!"* Then what would you think? Probably, *"Whoa, if I had known, I might have given a different answer!"*

Here's another example you may have actually experienced. You're with a group of friends in the lounge at school and one of them asks, *"What do you think of Joe?"* You hesitate, not knowing how to respond. If you say, *"I think Joe's a big jerk,"* your friend could say, *"I can't believe you said that. Joe's my best friend!"* Or if you say, *"I like Joe a lot,"* your friend might say, *"What are you thinking? He's done so many awful things to me!"* Aaaaaargh!

These are two examples of a convoluted form of communication we call "invisible," because it keeps the clarity and purpose of the communication invisible to the listener. It breeds confusion, mistrust and vagueness. To build trust, openness and quality in communication, you want to stay as visible as possible. Then you can choose to have the best possible chance of success in an interaction.

In Quantum Teaching, we use two tools that make communicating **visible** and **consistent.** Not only do we use them in our work, we also use them with our spouses, our colleagues and definitely with our students – inside the classroom and everywhere else. We teach them as mainstays, agreed-upon ways to handle communication. Those two tools are OTFD and the 4-Part Apology.

OTFD: Open the Front Door

We use this tool in situations where potential conflict exists. This approach resolves the conflict quickly and maintains the dignity of the listener. Then both parties can move on and maintain the relationship. Imagine the impact this could have with that certain student or colleague you've been struggling with. To help you remember the method and keep it in order, we call it Open The Front Door (OTFD). The metaphor reminds us to enter communication visibly through the front door.

Open = Observation

First, tell what happened in a completely objective, observable, fly-on-the-wall way to get both parties started at the same point. Example: *"I see you turned in all of your first four assignments*

late." Notice this is a statement of fact, not a judgment or conclusion. It's merely data.

The = Thought

Next, tell your thought or opinion using an "I" statement. Example: *"I'm thinking I may not have stated the deadlines or policies clearly, or that something is getting in the way of your turning your assignments in on time."*

Front = Feeling

Share your feeling, also in "I" form, (like I am sad, mad, glad... instead of This made me sad...). Example: *"When I saw that you hadn't done your assignments, I felt disappointed and frustrated."*

Door = Desire

State your intention, or the result you want. Example: *"I want you to get full credit for your work by turning it in on time, every time. Can we come up with a plan that will help you do that?"*

The beauty of this model is in its order. Without OTFD we usually end up hitting all of those areas, but not in a way that the other person can hear. Look what happens when . . .

We start with our **feeling:** *"I'm mad."* The other person instantly gets defensive, possibly without even knowing why we're mad.

We start with our **thought** or opinion: *"I think you're irresponsible."* The other person still gets defensive, wondering what right we have to make such a judgment, rather than on what may have happened to make us think that way.

We start with our **desire:** *"I think you should shape up or ship out."* Again, the other person gets defensive, thinking of what hurtful comeback to give us, rather than about the issue at hand.

By starting with the **observation,** the communication gets both people at the same starting point, listening with open minds. You can handle many misunderstandings right there in the first step. If you can't handle them at the first step, go through OTFD to facilitate the communication. We've found that taking the extra moment to organize our thoughts into this order also slows us down enough to word each part in a way that's calmer and easier to hear.

Where could this make a difference for you? We see it working wonders with spouses, colleagues, administrators, students and their parents. How about for you? Can you think of some people this might work with?

In addition to resolving conflicts, OTFD also works for communicating acknowledgments visibly. Want to acknowledge students in such a way that they can immediately internalize the association with their behavior and easily duplicate that behavior? As we pointed out earlier in the book, so many times we say things like, "Good job," "Nice," or "Way to go." While this leaves students feeling good, they don't always know why or what to do next time to earn the same praise. A student might think, "What's good, my writing or my penmanship?" Being visible with OTFD, you could say:

> *"When I noticed (O) that you used many descriptive words in your paragraph, I thought (T) it was easy to understand and picture what you were writing about. I'm delighted with (F) your descriptive writing and look forward to (D) more of it!"*

The 4-Part Apology

The second communication tool highlights the Key of Integrity. As much as you'd like to live your life in complete Integrity, it can be a challenge. Imagine the level of emotional and relational trust you can maintain when you quickly and authentically resolve mistakes. Apologizing when you've made a mistake isn't easy. When you and your students find yourselves in that situation, however, the 4-Part Apology can help. It allows you to acknowledge what you did, take responsibility for it, and look beyond the actual incident to the consequences of your behavior. By stating those consequences and choosing a different behavior, you can help the person you have affected move from feeling angry or resentful to being thoughtful and supportive. You can remember the four parts by this phrase: "It's All About My Relationships."

Re-word each of the following into OTFD form:

- "Good job!"
  On a test.

- "Great!"
  For putting supplies away.

- "Tsk-tsk"
  When student doesn't have homework ready to turn in.

Where could the 4-Part Apology make a difference for you with the following people:

- Spouse
- Teacher colleague
- Administrator
- Student
- Parent

A All = Acknowledge

Take responsibility for your actions by admitting them. Use "I" statements when speaking. *"I acknowledge that I didn't turn my homework in."*

A About = Apologize

State the cost or damage your actions caused. *"I apologize for breaking my word and frustrating you."*

M My = Make It Right

Deal with the consequences of the behavior and offer to make up for it with a solution. *"What can I do to make it right?"*

R Relationships = Recommit

Make a commitment to appropriate behavior which will mend the relationship. *"I agree to get all of my work in to you tomorrow and do my best to get future assignments in on time."*

People often think they're lowering themselves when they apologize for something they did or didn't do. Consequently, they feel frustrated. How many times have you been on the giving OR receiving end of an "I'm sorry," and felt incomplete?

Using the 4-Part Apology cleans up our mistakes and realigns our integrity. Model it first, and encourage your students to use this important life skill.

C BUILDING RELATIONSHIPS WITH AFFINITY

Imagine spending more time and energy reaching your students and less on "putting out fires." You can create a safe and inviting, yet challenging atmosphere where your students respect each other and work as a team.

We define "affinity" as closeness when applied to relationships. One exercise we use in our classes allows students a chance to get to know one another better. It is called the "Affinity Exercise" – an activity we learned from management consultant, Maggie Weiss. This activity opens doors for acknowledgments, enhancing esteem and confidence.

Consider the following interactions:

Teacher-Student

Do they have to like you? No. Does it make your work / life much easier? You bet. Does it add meaning on both ends? You bet.

Student-Student

Championship team dynamics require teammates to know, respect and have relationships with one another (Singer, 1993).

Teacher-Teacher

It's been said that education is one of the most isolated professions, yet what if we were a team? How much more of an impact could we make?

Lifelong Learner

As a student of life, do you need the ability to build rapport and affinity with tough students, tough teachers, tough bosses, and families?

You can use the Affinity Exercise in any or all of the following scenarios:

- In class, to build relationships as a team.

- In class, to give students guided practice focusing on themselves AND acknowledging others.

- With two students who've lost affinity due to conflict.

- With a family member, friend or colleague, to build or mend a relationship.

The Affinity Exercise

- Divide group into pairs.
- First person asks each of the following questions once, and responds to each answer with a simple "Thank You."

1 **Tell me something I don't know about you.**

2 **Tell me something you like about me.**

(If students don't know each other at all yet, you can change this to "something you like about yourself.")

3 **Tell me something we agree on.**

- Switch roles. Next person repeats the series of questions. Have the pairs do the exercise three times. People come up with something new every time and often it's the third round that has the most impact.

- Then change partners. This gives everyone a chance to talk to others on a more personal level.

During this activity, students find they share common interests and often form new understandings of and friendships with people. Even people who have known each other for a long time usually discover new aspects about one another.

REVIEW

In building the context for Quantum Teaching, personal skills help shape and orchestrate the atmosphere and foundation. You can create a strong foundation within your classroom by using and teaching visible communication, the 8 Keys, Living Above the Line and building Affinity. Clear communication and powerful life skills establish a safe, secure classroom environment, fostering greater risk-taking and ownership for learning.

THE AFFINITY EXERCISE

Tell me something –
- I don't know about you.
- You like about me.
- We agree on.

R E V I E W

Take a moment and envision the learning community you desire. Notice what your learners do, how they interact and what they say. Feel the sense of belonging, clarity, ownership and unity. Feel the excitement as students call upon one another to do their best, apply the 8 Keys and communicate powerfully through upsets and learnings.

What modeling will lead this kind of learning team? See yourself doing it. Become aware of your own ability and character to nurture powerful personal skills for successful living.

I Know!

Check the box if you know:

- ❏ How to Live Above the Line.
- ❏ The difference between Invisible and Visible communication.
- ❏ OTFD
- ❏ 4-Part Apology
- ❏ Affinity

 *Powerful Life Skills in your classroom!*

Orchestrating Success Through Implementation

chapter

10

What if it all worked?

ENROLL

What would happen if you implemented what you now know about orchestrating the atmosphere, foundation, environment, design, presentation and facilitation of curriculum using Quantum Teaching ideas and strategies?

Think about it. What *would* happen? Might it be uncomfortable? Maybe. Would you fail before you succeeded? Probably.

Would your students participate more? Change their attitudes about learning? Comprehend your curriculum better, apply it sooner, and retain it longer? You bet. Would you feel more energized? Inspired? Hopeful? Most likely. Would you feel more confident and competent? Sure. And finally, if you implemented what you know about orchestrating for student success, would school be a better place to come to?

a CHAPTER HIGHLIGHTS

REVIEW

Before we explore these possibilities, let's recap each chapter with a fast-forward, double-time review. Take a deep breath and let the following highlights summarize the material you've encountered.

1 Welcome!

You were introduced to the prime directive, Theirs to Ours, and the five tenets of Quantum Teaching: Everything Speaks, Everything is on Purpose, Experience Before Label; Acknowledge Every Effort; and If It's Worth Learning, It's Worth Celebrating. You also met Maestro and took your first look at the Design Frame, EEL Dr. C.

2 Atmosphere

The lead chapter in the Context section explored the necessary ingredients for a healthy and empowering atmosphere. You now know the importance of Intention, Rapport, Joy and

Wonder, Risk-taking, Belonging and Modeling within your classroom. Remember: everything speaks . . . always.

Foundation

You learned the roles of Purpose, Principles, Beliefs, Agreements, Policies, Procedures and Rules when you orchestrate the context for optimal learning. In addition, you discovered ways to keep your learning community growing, creating partnership and casting a strong vision of what's possible.

Environment

You learned ways to enhance your teaching through music, peripherals and the use of props, as well as the subtleties such as plants, aroma and seating.

Design

We expanded the prime directive, Theirs to Ours, emphasizing the need to "earn the right" to teach. Modalities, Multiple Intelligences and the Success Model refreshed the idea of Everything Is On Purpose. Then you gained a deeper understanding of Quantum Teaching's Design Frame, EEL Dr. C. Now you have your hands on the very core of orchestrating student success: Experience Before Label.

Presentation

This chapter began the second section called Content. Here you found answers to the question: "Am I a Quantum Teacher?" You added to your repertoire Modality Matching, Principles of Powerful Communication and congruent non-verbals. You then unwrapped the three Presentation Packages of Discoverer, Leader and Director. And finally, you discovered the impact of Anchoring.

Facilitation

We emphasized careful orchestration of the interactions present at the *moment* of learning. You tapped into KEG, and revisited the Success Model from a facilitator's viewpoint. You now can orchestrate students' states as well as smooth transitions using Influence Behavior through Actions. You encountered the Elicit Thinking Strategy and ways to debrief the moments learning happens.

Learning-to-Learn Skills

You grasped specific ways that enhance your students' abilities to learn quicker. Your students can discover their learning style and then apply that discovery to SLANT, note-taking (Mind Mapping and Notes:TM), studying (Circuit Learning), speed reading and memory.

Life Skills

You gathered ways that empower students to Live Above the Line; to take greater responsibility for the choices they make. Invisible communication was made visible using Open The Front Door, and integrity was restored with the 4-Part Apology – two powerful tools that bring clarity to your communication with others.

You've just completed the *short course* on Quantum Teaching. Although the first nine chapters are rich in useful applications, any one chapter could be explored and expanded in a full-day workshop. The fields of accelerated learning, cognitive psychology, neural science and educational best practices are immense. Perhaps it's more to know than you can possibly integrate into one class. Or is it? Teachers just like you, are implementing the principles and techniques of Quantum Teaching with solid results in public and private school classes, seminars, corporate training sessions and business presentations. You have joined a band of educators who have decided to meet challenges face on, shape students' lives and transform the system in which they work. Congratulations!

b THE MORNING AFTER

STEP 1:
Model

STEP 2:
Build unity

STEP 3:
Design and try it

STEP 4:
Evaluate and celebrate

Imagine: It's Monday morning. You arrive at school refreshed and energized from your reading of *Quantum Teaching*. Your head is buzzing. Affirmations from your "voice," new ideas for your classroom environment, and finer distinctions on how to design and deliver curriculum swim energetically in your mind as you walk briskly to your classroom. The key slips easily into the door and you enter aglow with possibilities. You wonder, "Where do I begin? What should I attempt first? Which of these hot ideas would be best to implement right now?"

First Thing

Share with your students what you're reading. Your enthusiasm is contagious! Explain the technique you're using and tell students the reason why. Let them in on the "secrets" of teaching and learning.

For some of you, sharing your knowledge of Quantum Teaching with colleagues may be met with skepticism. Your biggest weapon against colleague skepticism is your modeling. Begin successfully by implementing just one element of Quantum Teaching. You might choose music, posters, intention, the 8 Keys or even EEL Dr. C. Let your students and the results you achieve speak for you. Let your colleagues inquire about how you're now teaching more with less effort and your students are learning smarter, not working harder.

Monday and Tuesday

Build belonging and unity by validating student responses and really listening to each student when he/she speaks. Remember the triune brain research regarding the development of higher order thinking skills in the neo-cortex through safety and relationship in the limbic system.

Listen and watch. Observe how your students "show up." Look for the visual learners. Listen for the auditory learners. Feel for the kinesthetic learners. Then adjust your lesson and presentation to encompass all three modalities.

Celebrate successes. Often. Always. No matter how

small or insignificant they may seem to you.

Post affirmations signs such as "We learn when we risk," and "I am a gifted person."

Beginning Wednesday

Experiment with creating associations for a section of your content. Remember to tap into multiple sensory inputs (visual, auditory, kinesthetic) and the multiple intelligences. Connect the key concepts of your lesson to hand or body motions.

Establish traditions such as "Whooshes," "Whoa Clap," "Finger Snaps" or "Three Hoorays."

Note what went well these first few days. Celebrate your success.

In Preparation for the Following Week

Ask yourself, "What worked well this past week?" Pat yourself on the back as you practice *kaizen,* small seemingly insignificant, never-ending improvements.

If you haven't done so, take one lesson and design it so the students *experience* the content first before they attach the labels. Ask guiding questions that lead them to discover the principle idea, concept or strategy.

Remember to implement one Quantum Teaching element each week. Choose the one that you believe will produce the highest impact on student success. (And will stretch your comfort zone a bit!) Practice it until it's part of your natural repertoire. Keep stretching your comfort zone and expanding your resourcefulness. Notice the difference it makes as you model risk-taking for your learners.

> List the three elements you'll implement first

SEIZE THE OPPORTUNITY

The greatest gift you can give your students is the assurance that you're on their side, you want them to succeed and *together* you'll learn successfully. This camaraderie can't be measured, and won't show up on a standardized test score, but nothing counts without it.

Preparing students, at any age, to be lifelong learners

is an admirable goal; a goal toward which many have labored, yet few have consistently attained. The pressures from media, conflicting demands from within the educational system and wavering support from the community make the task even more challenging. However, despite the myriad distractions, one element remains at the center – **you.** You have the power to transform the lives of the ones who shape our future. Each day you look into the eyes, and hold the hearts and minds of people gifted with the blueprints of the future. Each day you orchestrate the interactions for dynamic learning. It's worth the risk and the challenge of implementing new ideas. It's worth the effort to rise above mediocrity. For the sake of our children, it's worth it. Do it.

You Know!

You *know* the essential elements to orchestrate student success, and you *know* you have the desire and ability to do it. Each day awaits the tremendous opportunity to shift students' perceptions of themselves as learners and stimulate their innate desire to learn. Seize the opportunity.

Have fun, and GO FOR IT!

Celebrate!

CELEBRATE

TOOLS, PROPS, MUSIC AND FUN!

This list is far from exhaustive. It's simply a short compilation of items we find useful. Read through the list with these thoughts in mind: "What could I use to enhance my students' ability to learn and comprehend the material? What would best elicit, support and maintain their state for learning?" As you read, allow your creativity to run free!

TOOLS

- "Boombox," a portable stereo system with CD capability
- "Marks-A-Lot" big markers
- "Mr. Sketch" markers
- Poster board for affirmation and truth signs
- Flip-chart stand and paper (or large newsprint, 2-hole punched at top and hung from the chalkboard with two large paper clips)
- Upright coat rack to hang costumes
- Toy box or old trunk for props
- Director's chair, tall

PROPS

- Arrow (practice-type with dull tip!)
- Picture frame
- Puppets
- Stuffed animals
- Basketball hoop
- "Koosh" Ball
- "Hackey" Sacks
- Juggling scarves
- "Z-bees" (a soft Frisbee)
- Masks: old person, clown, famous people
- Hats
- Director's "action" slate
- Wigs

MUSIC

- Initial instruction, studying, reading – Baroque: Flute, Piano or Violin.
- Special Effects – *TV's Greatest Hits*, Sound Effects
- Reflection, creating and designing projects – New Age Instrumental: Yanni, Arkenstone, Enya, Winston
- Breaks, entering, exiting the class – Popular Movie Soundtracks; *Greatest Hits of the 60's, 70's, 80's, 90's*; Contemporary Upbeat: solicit from your students
- Transitions – Contemporary Jazz, Reggae, Sing-Alongs

FUN

- Confetti and streamers
- Sparkling apple cider for celebrative toasts
- Balloons
- Noise makers
- Games: "Scrabble," "Pictionary," "Trivial Pursuit," "Nerf" Basketball, "Monopoly"
- *Book of Questions* for Kids
- Toys: "Legos," wooden blocks, dolls, cars, boats, airplanes
- Thinking Puzzles: "Rubik's Cubes," Tanagrams
- Clown nose, feet, hair, etc.

BIBLIOGRAPHY

chapter 1 Welcome

DePorter, Bobbi. (1992). *Quantum Learning.* New York: Dell Publishing.

Gazzaniga, Michael. (1992). *Nature's Mind.* New York: Basic Books.

Lozanov, Georgi. (November, 1978). "Suggestology and Suggestopedia." Paris: Paper presented to the United Nations Educational Scientific and Cultural Organization.

Vos-Groenendal, Jeannette. (1991). "An Accelerated/Integrated Learning Model Programme Evaluation: Based on Participant Perceptions of Standard Attitudinal and Achievement Changes." Dissertation [unpublished] ERIC and Northern Arizona University, Flagstaff, Arizona.

chapter 2 Atmosphere

Bandura, Albert. (May 8, 1988). *New York Times.*

Caine, Renate Nummela and Caine, Geoffrey. (1997). *Education on the Edge of Possibility.* Alexandria, Virginia: Association for Supervision and Curriculum Development, p. 124.

Csikszentmihalyi, Mihaly. (1990). *Flow - The Psychology of Optimal Experience.* New York: Harper Perennial. p. 4

Csikszentmihalyi, Mihaly. (March 4, 1986). "Concentration is Likened to Euphoric States of Mind." *New York Times.* p. C1.

Elkind, David and Sweet, Freddy. (May 1997). "The Socratic Approach to Character Education." *Educational Leadership* 54, 8:56-59.

Gardner, Howard. (1995). As interviewed by Daniel Goleman in *Emotional Intelligence.* New York: Bantam Books, p. 94.

Goleman, Daniel. (1995). *Emotional Intelligence.* New York: Bantam Books, p. 28.

LeDoux, Joseph. (1993). "Emotional Memory Systems in the Brain," *Behavioral and Brain Research,* p. 58.

LeDoux, Joseph. (June, 1994). "Emotion, Memory and the Brain," *Scientific American.* p. 50.

LeDoux, Joseph. (1992). "Emotion and the Limbic System Concept," *Concepts in Neuroscience,* p. 2.

Loomans, Diane and Kolberg, Karen. (1993). *The Laughing Classroom: Everyone's Guide to Teaching with Humor and Play.* Tiburon, California: H J Kramer, p. 153.

MacLean, Paul D. (1990). *The Triune Brain in Evolution.* New York: Plenum.

Seligman, Martin. (1991). *Learned Optimism.* New York: Knopf.

Singer, Blair. (1997). (Speaker). *Code of Honor.* Zephyr Cove, Nevada: Xcel. (Cassette Recordings)

Sylwester, Robert. (1995). *A Celebration of Neurons: An Educator's Guide to the Human Brain.* Alexandria, Virginia: Association for Supervision and Curriculum Development, p. 75.

Walberg, Herbert and Greenberg, Rebecca. (May, 1997). "Using the Learning Environment Inventory," *Educational Leadership* 54, 8:45-46.

Wells, Gordon. (1986). *The Meaning Makers: Children Learning Language and Using Language to Learn.* Portsmouth, New Hampshire: Heinemann Educational Books. p. 68.

chapter 3 Foundation

Caine, Renate Nummela and Caine, Geoffrey. (1997). *Education on the Edge of Possibility.* Alexandria, Va: Association for Supervision and Curriculum Development, pp. 159-160.

Dhority, Lynn. (1991). *The Act Approach.* Bremen, West Germany: PLS Verlag. p. 23.

Driscoll, Mary. (April 1994). "School Community and Teachers Work in Urban Settings: Identifying Challenges to Community in the School Organization." Paper presented at the annual meeting of the American Educational Research Association, New Orleans. Available through New York University. (From Caine, Renate Nummela and Caine, Geoffrey. (1997). *Education on the Edge of Possibility.* Alexandria, Va: Association for Supervision and Curriculum Development, p. 195.)

Hart, Leslie. (1983). *Human Brain, Human Learning.* New York: Freeman and Co., p. 109.

Magensen, Vernon. (Sept. 16, 1983). *Innovative Abstracts* 5:25 National Institute for Staff and Organizational Development, University of Texas, Austin, Texas.

chapter 4 Environment

Campbell, Don. (1997). *The Mozart Effect.* New York: Avon Books. p. 27.

Dhority, Lynn. (1991). *The ACT Approach: The Artful Use of Suggestion for Integrative Learning.* Bremen, Germany: PLS Verlag.

Dilts, Robert. (1983). *Roots of Neuro-Linguistic Programming.* Cupertino, California: Meta Publications.

Hirsch, A. (1993). "Floral Odor Increases Learning Ability." Presentation at annual conference of American Academy of Neurological & Orthopedic Surgery.

Lavabre, Marcel. (1990). *Aromatherapy Workbook.* Rochester, Vermont: Healing Arts Press.

Lozanov, G. (1979). *Suggestology and Outlines of Suggestopedia.* New York: Gordon and Breach Publishing. pp. 65-73

Lozanov, Georgi. (November, 1978). "Suggestology and Suggestopedia." Paper presented to the United Nations Educational Scientific and Cultural Organization.

Rose, Colin. (1985). *Accelerated Learning.* New York: Dell Publishing, p. 98.

Schuster, Don and Gritton, Charles. (1986). *Suggestive Accelerative Learning Techniques.* New York: Gordon and Breach Science Publishers.

chapter 5 Design

Boggeman, Sally, Hoerr, Tom and Wallach, Christine, eds. (1996). *Succeeding With Multiple Intelligences: Teaching through the Personal Intelligences.* St. Louis, Missouri: The New City School.

Gardner, Howard. (1983). *Frames of Mind: The Theory of Multiple Intelligences.* New York: Basic Books.

Gardner, Howard. (1991). *The Unschooled Mind: How Children Think and How Schools Should Teach.* New York: Basic Books.

Gardner, Howard. (1993). *Creating Minds.* New York: Basic Books. p. 104.

Grinder, John and Bandler, Richard. (1981). *Trance-formations.* Moab, Utah: Real People Press, p. 44.

Jensen, Eric. (1994). *The Learning Brain.* San Diego: Turning Point for Teachers.

Lakoff, George, and Johnson, Mark. (1980). *Metaphors We Live By.* Chicago: University of Chicago Press, p. 56.

Lozanov, Georgi. (November, 1978). "Suggestology and Suggestopedia." Paris: Paper presented to the United Nations Educational Scientific and Cultural Organization.

Markova, Dawna. (1992). *How Your Child is Smart: A Life-Changing Approach to Learning.* Berkeley, California: Conari Press.
Restak, Richard M. (1995). *Receptors.* New York: Bantam Books. p. 92.

chapter 6 Presentation

Grinder, Michael. (1991). *Righting the Educational Conveyor Belt.* Portland: Metamorphous Press, p. 165.
Lozanov, G. (1979). *Suggestology and Outlines of Suggestopedia.* New York: Gordon and Breach Publishing.

chapter 7 Facilitation

Armstrong, Thomas. (1994). *Multiple Intelligences in the Classroom.* Alexandria, Va: Association for Supervision and Curriculum Development. pp. 65-85.
Caine, Renate Nummela and Caine, Geoffrey. (1997). *Education on the Edge of Possibility.* Alexandria, Va: Association for Supervision and Curriculum Development.
Damasio, Antonio. (1994). *Descartes' Error.* New York: Grosset/Putnam.
Lazear, David. (1991). *Seven Kinds of Knowing: Teaching for the Multiple Intelligences.* Palatine, Illinois: Skylight Publishing.
Miller, George. (1956). "The Magical Number Seven Plus or Minus Two: Some Limits on Our Capacity for Processing Information." *Psychological Review* #63.

chapter 8 Learning Skills

Buzan, Tony. (1993). *The Mind Map Book.* New York: Dutton.
Damasio, Antonio. (1994). *Descartes' Error.* New York: Grosset/Putnam.
Ellis, Edwin. (1991). *SLANT: A Starter Strategy™ for Class Participation.* Lawrence, Kansas: Edge Enterprises.
MacLean, Paul D. (1990). *The Triune Brain in Evolution.* New York: Plenum.
Rose, Colin, and Nicholl, Malcolm. (1997). *Accelerated Learning for the 21st Century.* New York: Delacorte Press.
Schuster, Don and Gritton, Charles. (1986). *Suggestive Accelerative Learning Techniques.* New York: Gordon and Breach Science Publishers.

chapter 9 Life Skills

Singer, Blair. (1993). (Speaker). *How to Build a Championship Team.* Zephyr Cove, Nevada: Xcel. (Cassette Recordings).
Vos-Groenendal, Jeannette. (1991). "An Accelerated/Integrated Learning Model Programme Evaluation: Based on Participant Perceptions of Standard Attitudinal and Achievement Changes." Dissertation [unpublished] ERIC and Northern Arizona University, Flagstaff, Arizona.

RECOMMENDED READING

- Abernathy, Rob and Reardon, Mark. *Hot Tips: 25 Ways to Enhance Your Effectiveness as a Communicator.* Oceanside, CA: Firstborn Publications. 1997.

- Armstrong, Thomas. *7 Kinds of Smart.* New York: Plume/Penguin Books. 1993.

- Armstrong, Thomas. *Multiple Intelligences in the Classroom.* Alexandria, VA: Association of Supervision and Curriculum Development. 1993.

- Boggeman, Sally, Hoerr, Tom and Wallach, Christine, eds. *Succeeding With Multiple Intelligences: Teaching through the Personal Intelligences.* St. Louis, Missouri: The New City School. 1996.

- Buzan, Tony. *The Mind Map Book.* New York: Dutton. 1993.

- Caine, Renate Nummela and Caine, Geoffery. *Education on the Edge of Possibility.* Alexandria, VA: Association of Supervision and Curriculum Development. 1997.

- Campbell, Don. *The Mozart Effect.* New York: Avon Books. 1997

- Campbell, Linda, Campbell, Bruce and Dickinson, Dee. *Teaching and Learning Through Multiple Intelligences.* Needham Heights, MA: Allyn and Bacon. 1996.

- Canfield, Jack and Hansen, Mark Victor. *Chicken Soup for the Soul.* Deerfield Beach, FL: Health Communications, Inc. 1993.

- DePorter, Bobbi. *Quantum Business: Achieving Success Through Quantum Learning.* New York: Dell Publishing. 1997. *Quantum Learning: Unleashing the Genius in You.* New York: Dell Publishing. 1992.

- Dhority, Lynn. *The ACT Approach: The Artful Use of Suggestion for Integrative Learning.* Bremen, Germany: PLS Verlag. 1991.

- Dryden, Gordon and Vos, Jeannette. *The Learning Revolution.* Torrance, CA: Jalmar Press. 1994.

- Gardner, Howard. *Multiple Intelligences: The Theory in Practice.* New York: Basic Books. 1993.

- Glasser, William. *The Quality School: Managing Students Without Coercion.* New York: HarperPerennial. 1992.

- Goleman, Daniel. *Emotional Intelligences.* New York: Bantam Books. 1995.

- Grinder, Michael. *Righting the Educational Conveyor Belt.* Portland, OR: Metamorphous Press. 1991. *ENVoY: A Personal Guide to Classroom Management.* Battle Ground, WA: Michael Grinder and Associates, 1993.

- Hannaford, Carla. *Smart Moves.* Arlington, VA: Ocean Publishers. 1995.

- Harmin, Merrill. *Inspiring Active Learning.* Edwardsville, IL: Inspiring Strategies Institute. 1995.

- Hart, Leslie. *Human Brain, Human Learning.* New York: Brain Age Publishers. 1983.

- Herrmann, Ned. *The Creative Brain.* Lake Lure, NC: Brain Books. 1990.

- Jensen, Eric. *Brain-Based Learning.* Del Mar, CA: Turning Point for Teachers. 1996. *The Learning Brain.* San Diego: Turning Point for Teachers. 1995. *SuperTeaching.* Dubuque, IA: Kendall-Hunt. 1988.

- Kline, Peter. *The Everyday Genius.* Arlington, VA: Great Ocean Publishers. 1988.

- Kovalik, Susan and Olsen, Karen. *ITI: The Model: Integrated Thematic Instruction.* Kent, WA: Susan Kovalik and Associates. 1997.

- Lazear, David. *Seven Kinds of Knowing: Teaching for the Multiple Intelligences.* Palatine, IL: Skyline Publishing. 1991.

- Loomas, Diane and Kolberg, Karen. *The Laughing Classroom.* Tiburon, CA: HJ Kramer. 1993.

- Margulies, Nancy. *Mapping Inner Space.* Tucson, AZ: Zephyr Press. 1991.

- Markova, Dawna. *How Your Child is Smart.* Berkeley: Conari Press. 1992.

- McPhee, Doug. *Limitless Learning.* Tucson, AZ: Zephyr Press. 1996.

- Ostrander, Sheila and Schroeder, Lynn. *Super-Learning 2000.* New York: Delacorte Press. 1994.

- Rose, Colin and Nicholl, Malcolm. *Accelerated Learning for the 21st Century.* New York: Delacorte Press. 1997.

- Sims, Pamela. *Awakening Brilliance.* Atlanta: Bayhampton Publishers. 1997.

- Schuster, D. H. and Gritton, C.E. *Suggestive Accelerative Learning Techniques.* New York: Gordon and Breach Science Publishers. 1986.

- Sylwester, Robert. *A Celebration of Neurons.* Alexandria, VA: Association of Supervision and Curriculum Development. 1995.

INDEX

INDEX

implementing, 90–91
Explanation, 144–145
Eye
  contact, 124
  movement, 68

F
Facial expressions, 125
Facilitation
  audience, 150–151
  breaks, 154
  debriefing, 155–158
  definition, 5
  implementing, 108
  KEG, 144–146
  models, 146–150
  principles, 143–144
  short course, 212–213
  state, 151, 153
Feedback
  importance, 145–146
  negative, 196
Flow, definition, 23
Focus
  achieving, 183–184
  directing, 120
Foundation
  definition, 14
  short course, 212
Four-part apology, 203–204
Future-pacing, 58–59

G
Gardner, Dr. Howard
  flow, 23
  multiple intelligence, 4
  multiple intelligences, 96, 100
Gazzaniga, Dr. Michael, 11
Genius, tapping, 182–185
Gestures, 126–127
Glasper, Shereeta, 49
Goleman, Dr. Daniel, 22
Grinder, Dr. Michael, 4, 135
Grinder, John, 84
Gritton, Charles, 73, 173
Guidelines
  behavior, 45–46
  classroom, 56–57
  presentation, 114

H
Hahn, Kurt, 4
Hart, Leslie, 47
Higher Order Thinking Skills, 22
Hirsch, A., 72
Hopson, Leroy, 49, 53
HOTS, *see* Higher Order Thinking Skills
Hot tips spot, 136
Hunter, Madeline, 4

I
IBA, 152–153
Iconic posters, 68–69
Imagery, 103
Images
  classroom, 66
  eliciting, 119
Inclusiveness, 121–122
Information organizing, 175–182
Information processing, 120
Intelligence, *see* Multiple intelligences
  quotient, 96
Intention, 19–21
Interactions, 143
Interpersonal thinking, 97
Intrapersonal thinking, 98
Irvine, Kevin T., 137

J
Jensen, Eric, 103
Johnson, Mark, 4, 102
Justifying, 198

K
Kaizen, 138
KEG, 144–146
Kinesthetic alley, 136
Kinesthetic
  alley, 136
  assessment, 167
Kolberg, Karen, 27–28

L
Labeling
  definition, 10
  implementing, 91
Lakoff, George, 102
Language processing, 178

Lavabre, Marcel, 72
Leader, 130–131
Learning, *see also* Memory
  accelerated, 5
  beliefs about, 52–54
  belonging and, 36–38
  celebrating, 31–34
  celebration, 149
  circuit, 180–182
  classroom and, 18–19
  complexity, 3
  emotions and, 21–24
  environments, *see* Classrooms
  eye movement, 68
  partners, 57–58
  process, 29–30
  risk-taking, 34–36
  skills, short course, 213
  states, 150–151, 169–175
  styles, 165–169
Learning Forum, 4
LeDoux, Dr. Joseph, 22, 24
LeTellier, John, 102
Life skills
  importance, 195–197
  short course, 213
  tools, 200–206
  types, 197–200
Linguistic-verbal thinking, 97
Linking, 187–188
Location
  anchors, 134–137
  method, 188–190
Logical-mathematical thinking, 98
Loomans, Diane, 27–28
Lozanov, Dr. Georgi, 4
  alpha state, 173
  focus, 120
  modeling, 114
  teacher's role, 11
  teaching environment, 3
  theory, 65

M
MacLean, Dr. Paul D., 22, 172
Magnesen, Dr. Vernon A, 57
Markova, Dawna, 85
Memory, *see also* Learning
  imagery and, 103
  maximizing, 185–186

INDEX

Bobbi DePorter is President of Learning Forum, an Ocean-side, California-based company producing programs for students, teachers, schools and organizations across the United States as well as England, Hong Kong, Singapore and Malaysia.

Following a career in real estate investment, she co-founded an avant-garde business school for entrepreneurs that taught traditional business subjects in a non-traditional manner. She studied with Dr. Georgi Lozanov, the father of accelerated learning, and applied his methods to the school with great success. She later applied these techniques to the development of a program for teenagers called SuperCamp that opened in 1982, and founded Learning Forum, which has now helped over 25,000 students relearn how they learn and reshape how they live their lives. Results are well-documented, with students significantly increasing their grades, increasing participation and measurably feeling better about themselves. The success of SuperCamp's teaching methods led to invitations from schools and school districts to train teachers in these methods. These teacher-training courses evolved into Quantum Teaching, which is now being used by hundreds of teachers and integrated into schools and entire districts with great success. Bobbi is past president of the International Alliance for Learning and author of *Quantum Learning: Unleashing The Genius In You* and *Quantum Business: Achieving Success Through Quantum Learning.* Bobbi is the mother of two grown children. She and her husband, Joe Chapon, who is also her partner in Learning Forum, live and work in Oceanside, California.

Mark Reardon, M.S., is a past teacher and principal and now is internationally recognized as a lead facilitator for Learning Forum. His upbeat, inspiring presentations give a wealth of practical information and techniques designed to assist educators in becoming more valued, effective and successful professionals. He has personally trained thousands of educators in the public and private sectors.

Initially trained in Madeline Hunter's Elements of Effective Instruction and Clinical Supervision, he has been a project leader and demonstration teacher. He began training teachers and administrators after he completed the UCI Writing Project Summer Institute in 1984. Since that time Mark has co-founded Intertrainment, an educational consulting firm; taught at the internationally recognized accelerated learning program, SuperCamp; and presented for the National Staff Development Council's Annual Conference, the International Alliance for Learning, and the Association for Supervision and Curriculum Development's Professional Development Institutes. His audiences have included teachers, administrators, city officials, boards of education, international business people and students of all ages. He is founder of Centre•Pointe Education, co-founder of Firstborn Publications, and co-author of *Hot Tips: 25 Ways to Enhance Your Effectiveness as a Communicator.*

Mark lives with his wife, Lynn, and son, Noah, in Oceanside, California.

Sarah Singer-Nourie, M.A., is an award-winning teacher and trainer. She has touched the lives of thousands of students on the south side of Chicago, where she teaches Quantum Learning K-12 and high school English. There, and in both rural and urban schools across the country, she has brought new life to learning and motivational change for students, educators and business people from small groups to large conferences. Sarah is an internationally-recognized lead facilitator for Learning Forum, training thousands of teachers and learners all over the world through Quantum Programs and SuperCamp. She creates extensive training and development curricula, ranging from small projects to large system-wide initiatives for change which open possibilities in learning and growth for children and adults. She is president of Singer Learning Innovations, Inc.

Sarah and her husband, Colin Nourie, live in Chicago.

RESOURCES

LEARN MORE ABOUT QUANTUM TEACHING

Contact Learning Forum for a
FREE documentary video,
Quantum Teaching:
"Changing the Way We Learn!"

QUANTUM TEACHING™
QUANTUM LEARNING™

Staff Development
Teacher Inservices
Classroom Coaching
Student Programs

QUANTUM BUSINESS™

Corporate Culture
Train the Trainer

SUPERCAMP®

Learning-to-learn
and life skills youth
programs

SUCCESS PRODUCTS™

Books, videos
and audiotapes

LEARNING FORUM

1725 South Coast Highway   (800) 285-3276
Oceanside, CA 92054-5319   (760) 722-0072
Email: info@supercamp.com   (760) 722-3507 fax
www.supercamp.com

ASSOCIATIONS

ASSOCIATION FOR SUPERVISION AND
CURRICULUM DEVELOPMENT
1250 N. Pitt Street
Alexandria, VA 22314-1453

INTERNATIONAL ALLIANCE FOR LEARNING
1040 First Street
Encinitas, CA 92024

NATIONAL STAFF DEVELOPMENT COUNCIL
PO Box 240
Oxford, OH 45056